TEACHING OF CHEMISTRY

V. K. Bhalla

4263/3, Ansari Road,
Darya Ganj, New Delhi-110002

Published by:

SAURABH PUBLISHING HOUSE

Distributed by:

LOTUS PRESS

4263/3, Ansari Road, Darya Ganj, New Delhi-110002

Ph: 32903912, 23280047 • E-mail: lotus_press@sify.com

Saurabh Publishing is an imprint of

Lotus Press

Teaching of Chemistry

ISBN : 978-81-89005-52-8 (H/B)

Printed in India by Anand Sons, Delhi

Preface

The field of Chemistry is so broad that it would be foolhardy to undertake its coverage. Without trying to define the limits of the field, it is possible to divide this branch of chemistry into two approaches, the theoretical and the experimental. This book offers only an elementary approach for theoretical concepts for implementing the tools and techniques for effective teaching of chemistry.

Despite the description of this course as a study of special topics, an examination of the table of contents will disclose that the topics are not only related but more or less dependent upon each other. This book is teaching of chemistry, from its origins to the present time. The aim has been to provide a deeper and fuller understanding of the ideas and methods of the science by integrating the evolution of chemistry with the on march of history in general. The searching and experimentation of the past are so described that they may well provide both stimulation and special examples for solving present-day problems.

Investigators through the ages have contributed to our present-day knowledge of the nature of substances, affinity and chemical reactions. Throughout the volume, so far as possible, the story has been told by letting old records relate what actually took place. This has been done by making a careful and objective selection of pertinent material in early books and periodicals that are not readily accessible and from the professional papers, lectures, and letters of great chemists. In this way, the chronicle constructs a solid basis for interpreting the manifold connections between imagination and necessity, between theory and experiment.

The reader of these pages will soon discern that the development of chemistry has from earliest times gone hand in hand with progress in other sciences and philosophies, especially medicine, mineralogy, botany, zoology, physics, and engineering.

The scientific approach to reality consists of separating our experiences into simple parts so as to see them more clearly, and of connecting these parts so as to knowingly reconstruct what impressed us. This seems to be a complicated kind of approach. We use two steps, analysis and synthesis, and we have to create intricate relationships between them because separately they are contradictory and sterile.

It is an effort which has needed time for its development. The process is still going on. Itis accelerated pace does not seem to bring us closer to perfection. There is a meaningful irony in the fact that the more exact the methods of science which we develop, the more inaccessible does living reality appear to become. They are ageless parts of our culture. Science is always moving away from its past.

Thus time plays a dominant and continuous role in science, and history should therefore be an important part of the equipment which we use in continuing to build science.

Since this book is designed for undergraduate classroom study, a deliberate effort has been made to write it in a language suited to its purpose. Also, I have not hesitated to use elementary explanations for many controversial ideas. It is my belief that the ever-changing nature of chemistry will make many of these concepts obsolete within too short a period of time.

Many persons including various friends, colleagues, and students in chemistry have contributed to this book. It is impossible to give each of them the credit that is due. Without their searching and helpful criticism many misstatements and ambiguities would have escaped into the final text.

Author

Contents

1

Foundation of Chemistry: Atoms and Molecules

Introduction

When chemical change was explained not by ìhidden qualitiesî but by mere repulsions and attractions, electrical charge offered a persuading reason. In the theory of Jean-Theophile des Aguliers, the ardent disciple of Newton, particles of air repel one another because they are charged with positive electricity. Sulfurous, that is combustible, particles also repel one another, but they do it because of a negative charge. The attraction between air and combustible particles combines them into electrically neutral *moleculae*. The assumption of the electrically opposite nature of charges supported the concept of atoms by connecting an impressive new property with them.

This thought was carried to its philosophical extreme by Roger Josephus Boscovish (1711-1787) who taught in Italy and in France. He combined Newtonís theory of forces which act at a distance, with Leibnizís thoughts of monads as simplest elements. The transfer of motion from one body to another in collision is so difficult to represent for material atoms that a new hypothesis was required, one which abolished the dualism of matter and force altogether. Atoms then become mere geometric points, centers of force, and nothing else. They produce attraction at a measurably large distance, in accordance with the laws of gravitation. At a very small, immeasurable distance, the force is repulsive and becomes infinitely large as the distance diminishes to infinitely small. These properties of the force, which are again reversed at very great distances, actually constitute what is commonly called space and all qualities of matter can be derived from it.

This dynamic theory of matter replaced the discontinuity of discrete atoms by continuous force. Kant at one time called the atom ìa mere idea.î It was more than that to the Abbe Rene Juste Hauy, since he felt that he had opened a physical approach to the realm of the atom. Crystals of Iceland spar can be split in such manner that the smaller fragments retain the same rhomobohedrical arrangements of planes and angles which characterize the natural specimen.

This must be due to a regular arrangement not only of the spar but also of every smallest particle. A crystal consists of a nucleus and enveloping matter of molecules which have the same form as the nucleus, superimposed upon it according to definite rules. Although Torbern Bergman had already noted the ìnatural jointsî or planes of easy rupture in some crystals, Hauy was at first derisively called the crystalloclast ìcrystal splitter.î He continued, nevertheless, in his efforts, and arrived at the foundations of a law of definite geometric proportions characterizing the situation of the planes of a crystal.

Hauyís crystallographic theory was the basis for C.S. Weiss (1780-1856, Berlin), from which he constructed ìthe natural subdivisions of the crystal systemsî (1815). Atoms were not necessary for this enterprise; Weiss rejected atomism in favor of dynamism. It had become a fashion, in a sometimes outspoken rivalry between French and German scientists, to consider atomistic theory as the field of the French and the ìdeeperî dynamistic theory as essentially German. In England, at that time, William Higgins (1766-1825) and, a few years later, John Dalton (1766-1844, Manchester), explored the meaning of atomism for chemistry.

Higgins based his opinions upon the work on specific gravities and the attractive powers of various salt solutions, and particularly on the composition of nitrous air, of Richard Kirwan (1733-1812, Dublin) who received the Copley medal from the Royal Society in 1782. Adhering to Kirwanís phlogistical viewpoint, Higgins theorized: ìNitrous air, according to Kirwan, contains 2 of dephlogisticated to 1 of phlogisticated air. I am of opinion that every primary particle of phlogisticated air is united to two of dephlogisticated air, and that these molecules are surrounded with a common atmosphere of fire.î Then, further following the trend of usingî numbers to designate the relative magnitudes of affinities, he ìsupposesî that not more than five particles of dephlogisticated air (oxygen) can combine with one of phlogisticated air (nitrogen), towards which the former will gravitate ìas their common center of gravity. This is the most perfect state of colourless nitrous acid.î

John Dalton sought an explanation for Priestleyís and his own finding that the composition of the atmosphere is the same at different heights. Oxygen and nitrogen differ in specific gravity; why does this not cause a separation of the two? In the autumn of 1801 ìI hit upon an ideaî that ìthe particles of one gas are not elastic or repulsive to the particles of another gas, but only to the particles of their own kind.î These particles consist ìof the supposed impenetrable nucleus, together with its surrounding repulsive atmosphere of heat.î Since it is not known that the specific gravities of substances vary, ìwe may conclude that the ultimate particles of all homogeneous bodies are perfectly alike in weight, figure, etc.î The proportions of weights in a compound are the proportions of the weights of the atoms. Lavoisier found 85 per cent of oxygen and 15 per cent of hydrogen in water; therefore an atom of oxygen is 5.66 times the weight of an atom of hydrogen. In ammonia, 80 per cent of nitrogen is combined with 20 per cent of hydrogen; therefore a nitrogen atom weighs four times as much as a hydrogen atom. The assumption that one atom of each element is present in the compound is made by Dalton without any further explanation.

Wherc thcre are two different compounds between the same elements, the atoms are assumed to combine in a 1-to-1 relationship in one of them, and in a 1-to-2 proportion in the other.

There are two compounds of hydrogen with sulphur; the one, a wellknown elastic fluid denominated ësulphuretted hydrogen,í the other a viscid, oily compound called ësupersulphuretted hydrogen.í The former consists of 1 atom of each element, the latter probably of 1 atom of hydrogen united to 2 of sulphur.

1. Sulphuretted hydrogen

The best way I have found to obtain sulphuretted hydrogen in a pure state is to heat a piece of iron to a white or welding heat in a smithís forge, then suddenly drawing it from the fire, apply a roll of sulphur.

Sulphuretted hydrogen is unfit for respiration and for supporting combustion. . . . Water absorbs just its bulk of this gas; when, therefore, it is mixed with hydrogen, this last will be left after washing in water, or what is still better, in lime water. Sulphuretted hydrogen burns with a blue flame. When mixed with oxygen, in the ratio of 100 measures to 50 of oxygen (which is the least effective quantity), it explodes by an electric spark; water is produced, sulphur deposited, and the gases disappear. If 150 or more measures of oxygen are used, then after the explosion over mercury, about 87 measures of sulphurous acid are found in the tube, and 150 of oxygen disappear, or enter into combination with both the elements of the gas.

From these facts, the constitution of sulphuretted hydrogen is clearly pointed out. It is 1 atom of sulphur and 1 of hydrogen, united in the same volume as 1 of pure hydrogen. When burned, 2 atoms of oxygen unite to 1 of sulphur to form sulphurous acid, and 1 of oxygen to 1 of hydrogen to form water. The weights of elements confirm this constitution. One atom of sulphur has been found to weigh 13, to which adding 1 for hydrogen, we obtain the weight of an atom of sulphuretted hydrogen = 14; this number likewise expresses the number of times that sulphuretted hydrogen should exceed hydrogen in specific gravity. But common air exceeds hydrogen 12 times: therefore, 12:14::specific gravity of common air; specific gravity of sulphuretted hydrogen = 1.16, agreeably to the preceding determination. Hence this gas is wholly composed of sulphur and hydrogen, as above.

2. Supersulphuretted Hydrogen

When liquid alkali is poured upon supersuphuretted hydrogen, heat is produced, hydrosulphuret is formed, and sulphur precipitated.

OXYGEN WITH SULPHUR

1. Sulphurous Oxide

When sulphuretted hydrogen gas and sulphurous acid gas are mixed over mercury, in the proportion of 6 measures of the former to 5 of the latter, both gases lose their elasticity, and a solid deposit is made on the sides of the tube. The common explanation given of this fact is, that the hydrogen of the one gas unites to the oxygen of the other to form water, and the sulphur of both gases is precipitated. This explanation is not correct; water is indeed formed, as is stated; but the deposition consists of a mixture of two solid bodies, the one sulphur, the other sulphurous oxide; they may be distinguished. It will appear in the sequel that 5 measures of sulphuric acid contain twice as much oxygen as the hydrogen in 6 measures of sulphuretted hydrogen require.

As far, then, as appears, sulphurous oxide is a compound of one atom of sulphur and one of oxygen; it is capable of combining with muriatic, and perhaps other acids; when suspended in water, it gives it a milky appearance and a bitter taste, and the mixture being heated, the oxide is changed into sulphur and sulphuric acid. An atom of sulphur being estimated, from other considerations hereafter to be mentioned, to weigh 13, and one of oxygen weighing 7, it will follow that oxide of sulphur is constituted of 65 per cent sulphur and 35 per cent oxygen.

Carbon forms two oxides: the first, carbon oxide, contains one atom each of carbon and oxygen; the second, carbon dioxide, has two atoms of oxygen for one of carbon. Since Lavoisier, after several modifications, finally arrived at 72 per cent of oxygen and 28 per cent of carbon in the dioxide, and since the atomic weight of oxygen was derived from the composition of water to be 5.66, the atomic weight of carbon was 4.4, calculated from the proportion $72 : 28 = (2 \times 5.66) : x$

In 1803 Dalton combined these values in a table of atomic weights which he subsequently corrected and enlarged. He used several kinds of graphical representations of atoms. A small circle, surrounding the initial of the element as the heat atmosphere surrounds the atomic nucleus, designates the atom.? zinc = C = copper Oxygen is designated by an empty circle, carbon by a black circle.

Two gaseous compounds of carbon with hydrogen had been investigated at that time, marsh gas and olefiant gas. Volta described the sky-blue flame with which marsh gas burns. This distinguishes it from hydrogen and indicates that its presence is the cause of all flames. Whether paper or wood or alcohol are the burning substances, they are first converted into marsh gas and only then do they give a flame.

Olefiant gas was obtained when the four Dutch chemists, Deiman, Paets van Troostwyk, Bondt and Lauwerenburg, heated alcohol with a large quantity of sulphuric acid. Its name was chosen to characterize its property of forming an oil when it combines with chlorine. The proportions of carbon to hydrogen are 75: 25 in marsh gas, 85.7: 14.3 in olefiant gas. Dalton saw that this means 6: 2 in the first, and, closely enough, 6: 1 in the second. The discrepancy between the atomic weight 6 here found and 4.4 previously calculated for carbon was not considered critical; Dalton knew that these experimental results were open to great improvement.

Dalton originally intended the theory only for materials ìin the state of a pure elastic fluid.î In 1810 he extended the atomic theory to solid substances like metals because they react with gases and should, therefore, offer the same kind of ultimate particle.

Daltonís work was not too kindly received by Davy. He wrote to Berzelius, who had asked his opinion about it, as follows:

> It is not a little curious that the first views of the Atomic Chemistry, which has been so much expanded by Dalton and generally in my opinion after ideas more ingenious than correct, are to be found in a work published in 1789 by William Higgins, A Comparative View of the Two Theories of Chemistry.

It is true that Higgins indicated a law of multiple proportions and a heat atmosphere surrounding the atom. These are essential aspects which recurred in Daltonís theory but they were here amplified by more definite examples and a wider range of applications than Higgins found. Besides that, Daltonís sign language brought the philosophical thought into the form of a chemical theory. If this seemed ìmore ingenious than correctî to Davy, it was greatly stimulating to his friend and mentor in scientific methods, William Hyde Wollaston. He gave the ìdirectest proofî of the law of multiple proportions by simple experiments with potassium salts. Potassium forms two kinds of salts with sulfuric acid, a supersulfate (bisulfate) and a neutral sulfate. The former is obtained by heating potassium carbonate with an excess of sulfuric acid until the free acid is evaporated. When twenty grams of carbonate were used in this operation, it required just twenty more grams of the carbonate to convert the bisulfate into the neutral salt. By a somewhat different method, the proof for the oxalates was just as simple. Take two equal quantities of the super oxalate and burn the oxalic acid in one of them. The ash obtained is just sufficient to convert the other portion into the neutral oxalate. The supersalts thus contain one part of the alkali for one of the acid, the neutral salts two parts of the alkali for one of the acid. In the quadroxalate, the proportion is four acid to one alkali.

All this could be expressed in Proustís theory without using atomic concepts. For Wollaston, arithmetical relations were insufficient; he needed further explanation for a complete chemical theory. With the new theory it became possible to construct models for the chemical compounds. When the proportion of atoms in a compound is 4 : 1, the four can be placed in the corners of a regular tetrahedron.

Besides leading to such appealing structural models, the theory also provided a basis for the critical evaluation of experimental results. When Berzelius became acquainted with Daltonís theory, he found that it confirmed the analyses of salts which he had been carrying on since 1807. He saw in Daltonís theory ìone of the greatest advancesî of chemistry, although he reproached its author for leaving too little for the experiment to decide and for having had ìtoo little distrust in his own way of applying the hypotheses to the systemî (1818). Differences between predictions of the theory and the results of experimental measurements arose in the further progress of Berzeliusí work. This stimulated him to repeat and to modify the procedures. ìEnlightened by the knowledge of my own errors, and with the aid of better methods, I finally found a great accord between the results of the analyses and the calculations of the theory.î

It was quite difficult to determine atomic weights. Dalton gave for sulfur figures which varied from 17 and 14.4 in 1803 to 22 and 12 in 1806. Obviously, without the guidance of a theory, experiments alone would not have led to the conclusion that particles of constant weight exist. Therefore it came as a great and even unbelievable surprise when Gay-Lussac found that the chemical combinations of gases always occur in simple volumetric proportions. Joseph Louis Gay- Lussac himself was prepared for such uniform behavior of gases. He had discovered that all gases have the same coefficient of thermal expansion so that when two substances in gas form had the same volume at one temperature, the volumes remained equal to each other at all temperatures. When he reinvestigated the water reaction, for which Cavendish and Priestley already had indicated simple volumetric proportions, he stated that, by volume, 2 hydrogen combine with 1 oxygen to form 2 water vapor. That he did this work in collaboration with Alexander von Humboldt was because of an unusual reason. The great German explorer, recently returned to Paris from his travels in South America, had published measurements of the oxygen content in air which Gay-Lussac criticized very sharply. Instead of resenting this, Humboldt sought friendship with the younger man and better chemist.

Simple volumetric proportions were also found for the formation of carbon dioxide, nitrogen oxides, and ammonia:

2 carbon oxide + 1 oxygen = 2 carbon dioxide by volume

3 hydrogen + 1 nitrogen = 2 ammonia

The neutralization of ammonia by carbon dioxide, or by hydrochloric acid, again showed such simple volumetric relations. Gay Lussac concluded that similar simple relations would be found if the components of all salts were obtainable in gas form.

Dalton immediately raised two objections to Gay-Lussacís experiments and generalizations. The first objection was directed against the accuracy of the volumetric measurements. Dalton, who had found no difficulty in accepting widely varying figures for the atomic weights of carbon or of sulfur, now insisted that not 2 but 1.97 volumes of hydrogen combined with 1 volume of oxygen, and that this deviation was sufficient to invalidate the law. The second objection was more fundamental. Gay-Lussacís law would necessarily lead to the conclusion that equal volumes of gases contained equal numbers of atoms. Dalton had tried and rejected this assumption.

Actually, the volume does not change in this reaction. This means that Gay-Lussacís law had to be rejected on the basis of the theory which assumed that the atoms in nitrogen and oxygen as elements were simple, while the atoms of nitrogen oxide were complex, just as the graphic models showed. Was this theory more reliable than the measurements? Or was it possible to modify the theoretical concept so that it would be consistent with the experimental results?

Amadeo Avogadro assumed that in all gases, whether they are elements or compounds, the ultimate particles are complex. In his language, the particles always consist of a certain number of integral molecules united by attraction. The process of chemical combination, which in Daltonís theory was a simple addition of atoms, involves a step in which the molecules actually present are divided into integral molecules. The particles in nitrogen and oxygen gas consist of two integral molecules. The twins are split when the chemical combination brings one integral molecule each of nitrogen and oxygen together to form the new particle of the nitrous gas. With an oxygen particle which consists of two integral molecules, as shown by this reaction, the formation of water must be explained as follows: Four integral molecules of hydrogen combine with two of oxygen into two molecules of water. Each particle of water then contains one integral molecule of oxygen with two of hydrogen, and if the atomic weight of hydrogen is defined as 1, that of oxygen must be 15 (according to the best value at that time). It was Daltonís error to assume, from the proportions of the weights of oxygen and hydrogen in water, that the atom of oxygen was 7.5. Unfortunately, after pointing out this error, Avogadro committed it himself at the end of his exposition.

Gay-Lussacís law the ìFrench doctrine,î as it was called, which the Englishman Dalton said he could not ìadmit,î was thus reconciled with an enlarged atom theory by the Italian Avogadro. He did not make it sufficiently clear, however, that atoms must be distinguished from molecules, which are ìparticlesî consisting of several atoms. This may explain why his theory found little acceptance.

The uniform behaviour of all gases, the simplicity of the relationships between volume, temperature, and pressure, indicated to the physicist AndrÈ Marie AmpËre (1775-1836, Paris) that equal volumes of gases contain equal numbers of molecules. The spaces between them are infinitely large compared with the size of the molecules themselves. The chemically active particle is not the smallest unit; it is composed of several, physical molecules, at least of four. Chlorine, for example, must consist of at least eight physical molecules in one chemical particle.

This distinction between physical and chemical ultimate units was not revolutionary. It had a model in the clusters of matter which Robert Boyle had vaguely described. Ampre speculated about the arrangements of these molecules in geometrical forms. Wollaston published similar thoughts shortly before Ampere. Neither impressed the chemists of their time. General theories needed experimental evidence, even if the evidence was quite limited, at least in the beginning. Nor was the idea that atoms consist of smaller units entirely abhorrent. The thought expressed in 1815 and 1816 by the English doctor, William Prout, that all elements are ultimately composed of hydrogen units did not cause any great astonishment. At that time atoms and molecules still belonged more to philosophy than to physics and chemistry.

Avogadro again presented his views in 1818; AmpËre explained his theory once more in 1835. Jean-Baptiste Andre Dumas (1800-1884) measured the density of gases of mercury, phosphorus, and other substances which require high temperatures for vaporization, and at first (1827) thought that his results could be explained by Avogadroís and AmpËreís theories. Later on, in 1837, he declared that he would like to ban the word atom from chemistry because it indicates something which is beyond the reach of chemical experience.

2

Chemistry Education: Theory and Practice

Introduction

Many students enter their undergraduate chemistry courses with no experience in chemistry at all or, at most, a one-year high school course in chemistry. Many enter so-called non-major courses in chemistry with the intention of fulfilling a requirement, whether for a liberal-arts degree; for engineering, nursing, or physical-therapy degrees; or for the fulfilment of requirements for premedical, predental, and biological-science programs. A very small minority enters these courses as declared majors in chemistry or biochemistry. In every case, the prior chemical experience of these students is very uneven, ranging from minimal to no chemistry to several years of guided research.

Although recent literature in chemical education tends to give major attention to introductory chemistry courses designed for the students identified above, chemistry education also takes place in the subsequent years of the undergraduate curriculum, from courses in organic chemistry and physical chemistry to advanced courses that serve both undergraduate and graduate students.

The Introductory College Chemistry Course

In USA, the attention given to introductory college chemistry is well deserved and will be the focus of the remainder of this chapter. Indeed, Project Kaleidoscope, in its monograph ìWhat Works: Building Natural Science Communities,î states unequivocally that the transformation of introductory courses must be the National Science Foundationís highest priority over the next five years since a significant body of research confirms that the first year of college is the critical drop-off point in numbers of students in science and mathematics courses and that students acquire and confirm lifelong beliefs and attitudes about science and mathematics in their introductory courses. Until recently, very few alternatives to the ìtraditionalî general chemistry course could be found in the undergraduate chemistry curriculum either in major or non major courses. Brock Spencer, in his 1991 Chemical Manufacturers Association Catalyst Award address, ìWhat Works in Chemistry Education,î aptly described this traditional course an unrelated set of problems to be worked by choosing the right formula to apply, a three-hour lab to be endured in which the purpose is to come as close as possible to the ërightí answer, and an occasional multiple choice exam. Students view the material as a set of isolated exercises to be solved rather than as part of an exciting conceptual structure, as preparation for the next course rather than as preparation to understand the world, and as an impersonal, competitive and isolating experience.

The non major course was often taught as simply a less rigorous version of the major course, but with the same emphasis, as Sheila Tobias has reported in ìTheyíre Not Dumb, Theyíre Differentî regarding dry, factual, predigested rule-ordered material. And all this in lecture halls containing two- to five hundred students and in laboratories (when they exist) supervised by graduate students with minimal instruction in pedagogical skills. Thatís the bad news. The good news is that something is being done about it. Spencer has cited the many different models that are currently being tried in many kinds of institutions. These models include:

- New introductory courses that pose and solve real experimental problems in an investigative approach to chemistry using modern instruments;
- Courses that provide direct laboratory experience with phenomena first, followed by development of concepts based on those investigations;
- Courses that coordinate content with other science courses, so that students see connections among several disciplines;
- Courses that feature varied methodologies such as peer learning, concept development rather than topic coverage, classroom attention to current scientific literature, and societal and personal issues.

The initiatives described by Spencer come at a time that the American Chemical Society, through the agency of some of its branches, is attempting to support curricular change in introductory chemistry courses. Recognizing that undergraduate courses must support the educational needs and career aspirations of future citizens as well as future scientists, the ACS has recommended that

- introductory chemistry courses be redesigned in order to rekindle student interest and address the specific needs of unprepared students;
- current efforts to develop a scientifically literate citizenry be expanded;
- the reward structures of colleges and universities include incentives for quality instruction and provide opportunities for faculty growth and development;

- strategies and incentives be developed to encourage the entry of underrepresented populations into chemistry;
- Major laboratory curriculum development address the needs of undergraduate institutions to upgrade instructional equipment, provide hands-on chemistry experiences for all undergraduates, and establish more undergraduate research opportunities for chemistry majors.

Some Specific Initiatives in Chemistry Education

Two specific initiatives, one addressing the major course and one addressing the non major course, am described below.

The Task Force on General Chemistry. Several years ago, recognizing the critical need to address the specific issue of general chemistry courses for the career-related disciplines of the majors and sciences, Stanley Kirschner, thenchair of the Division of Chemical Education, in USA ACS, established a Task Force on General Chemistry. Members of the Task Force believed that general chemistry needed to be revitalized and were concerned with both content and process of what was taught and how it was taught. The Task Force was composed of three subcommittees to carry out its charge from three different points of view: a modular/core curricular approach, a subject-area approach, and a laboratory based approach. Although the Task Force agreed that there was not one ìbestî approach to teaching general chemistry, it also felt that general chemistry needed to be unburdened from its present abundance of detail and incoherence. The Task Forceís focus was to develop a curriculum suited to all introductory chemistry students in two-year and four-year colleges.

ìChemistry in Context.î The ACS is also sponsoring the development of a new college chemistry textbook entitled *Chemistry in Context: Applying Chemistry to Society*, edited by

A. Truman Schwartz, intended primarily for students who do not anticipate majors or careers in chemistry or other sciences. The primary goal of *Chemistry in Context* is to motivate students to learn chemistry so that they can and will act as responsible citizens in our increasingly technical age. The text has been structured in such a way that students will discover the theoretical and practical significance of chemistry and will also become aware of what a very human endeavor chemistry is. In this textbook a broad range of group and individual activities has as its object the empowerment of students so that they can locate information, and develop analytical skills, critical judgment, and the ability to assess risks and benefits.

The initiatives cited above address the urgent need articulated by Bassam Z. Shakhashiri:

> In our advanced scientific and technological society, we must pay special attention to the science and technology education of the non-specialist. Our scientific enterprise and, indeed, our well-being as a society will be doomed unless we quickly develop a literate citizenry one that can distinguish between astronomy and astrology; that can deal successfully with the complex issues related to animals' rights; that can benefit from advances in the nutritional sciences; that can deal responsibly with pollution and pollution control; and that can appreciate the benefits of chemicals, their potential hazards, their safe handling, and their disposal. The very democratic principles upon which our society was founded and continues to function are now seriously threatened and will be jeopardized unless we achieve a state of literacy in science, mathematics, and technology. Literacy in those fields is a measure of our values as a society: what we are about, what we believe in, how we treat each other, and how we treat our plane.

Theory

Over the past fifty years, research in chemistry teaching has revealed that a vast majority of chemistry students at all levels, including the graduate level, learn chemistry concepts by rote and solve chemistry problems by using algorithmic methods. Although many students perform satisfactorily on exams, it has been found that interviews with students can reveal gross misconceptions regarding chemical phenomena. The insights into student learning outlined below can help instructors rethink the teaching process so that they can teach for meaning and not simple rote playback of chemical concepts.

Piaget and Chemistry Teaching

Herron breakthrough paper applies Piagetís theories on how we acquire knowledge to the teaching of chemistry. Piaget distinguished among four stages of intellectual development: the sensory-motor, preoperational, concrete operational, and formal-operational stages. The concrete-operational student structures and organizes activity in reference to concrete things and events in the immediate present. Such a student does not think in terms of possibilities and is not able to understand abstract concepts that depart from concrete reality. The formal-operational student, on the other hand, thinksóor at least is beginning to thinkóin terms of what might happen and envisions all the changes that are possible. Formal-operational students can reason without the aid of visual props.

Although the instructional approach that we take and virtually every concept that we teach in chemistry requires learners to be at the formal operational level (normally reached by age fifteen, according to Piaget) if they are to comprehend the concepts that are presented, a widely publicized study done at the University of Oklahoma indicated that only 50 per cent of the college freshmen who were tested functioned completely at the concrete operational level and that only 25 per cent of the sample could be considered fully formal in their thought processes. Such statistics should have tremendous influence on how we teach chemistry.

Herron has suggested that we confront the problem of delivery of chemical concepts to concrete-operational students in one of two ways: either skirt the problem or overcome it. Skirting the problem involves making formal concepts accessible to concrete-operational students by emphasizing concrete concepts and testing for their mastery. Overcoming the problem involves taking steps to enable concrete conceptualizers to develop into formal thinkers at some later time. One suggestion that Herron has offered is that we can help students acquire surrogate concepts that can substitute for the real thing by providing extensive experience with concrete props that model the abstract concept. The hope is that the transition from the surrogate to the real will become increasingly easy as the student matures. This transition can be encouraged if students are forced to think about what they are doing, are engaged in the intellectual debate of ideas, are required to weigh evidence, and are helped to make sense of a series of observed facts. Although provision of these educational experiences is often frustrating and time consuming and requires a great deal of interaction among students and between student and teacher, instructors can make considerable progress in chemistry teaching if they take the time to provide some of these experiences.

Constructivism: A Theory of Knowledge

According to Bodner, the constructivist model of learning can be succinctly summarized by the statement: Knowledge is constructed in the mind of the learner. This idea is a logical outgrowth of Piagetís model of intellectual development, since his model was built upon the assumption that knowledge is constructed as learners strive to organize their experiences in the framework of preexisting mental structures. The constructivist model can be summarized as follows:

- It can be very helpful in explaining and overcoming student misconceptions, which are so resistant to instruction that the only way to replace a misconception is to help students construct a new concept that more appropriately explains the experience.

- It has some important implications for instruction. For the instructor it requires a subtle shift in perspective from someone who ìteachesî to someone who tries to facilitate learning: a shift from teaching by imposition to teaching by negotiation.
- It facilitates a two-directional flow of information between student and teacherówhich, in turn, requires students to explain their answers, to reflect on their learning process, and to be responsible for the language they use.
- It is a paradigm of the basic scientific-research process.

Table 2.1. Summary of Characteristics of the Traditional View and the Constructivist View of Learning

Traditional View	Constructivist View
Reality is a static body of knowledge	Construction is a process in which knowledge is both built and continually tested
Mind is a black box	Environment is a black box
Stimulus-response is accurately judged	Mental process is accurately judged
Mental process is guessed at	Relationship between mental structures and real world is guessed at
Learners mirror and reflect what they hear and read	Learners construct own knowledge by looking for meaning and order
Learning is more passive	Learning is more active
There is a search for a match with reality	There is a search for a fit with reality (lock and key analogy)
Copies or replicas of reality are in learners' minds	Many keys with different shapes can open a given lock

Developmental Instruction: Application of the Perry Model to General Chemistry

The realization that students are active learners with various stages of intellectual, emotional, and ethical maturity can and should have a profound effect on the methods that instructors use for teaching and the environments that they create for learning. A cognitive development model that seems useful to chemistry educators is that described by William Perry. David Finster has shown how the various stages, or positions, of intellectual and ethical development in college students within the Perry model can be related to how students learn chemistry. Perryís scheme of development can be grouped into four categories dualism, multiplicity, relativism, and commitment to relativism each of which represents a unique way of thinking or a particular cognitive filter through which students understand their world.

Table 2.2. Relationship of Perry Categories to Student Responses to an Introductory Lecture on Chemical Bonding

Perry Category	Student Response
Dualism: The student sees the world in terms of opposites: good-bad, right-wrong, we-they. Truth is absolute; uncertainty is only temporary.	Student enjoyed lecture on chemical bonding because professor conveyed air of authority. Student was confused because the advantages and disadvantages of each theory were summarized, but the teacher never said which theory was "right."
Multiplism: Diversity and uncertainty are legitimate; all opinions are equal, including those of authorities.	Student enjoyed hearing about different approaches to bonding; dilemma is trying to guess which approach the teacher thinks is right.
Relativism: Student recognizes that knowledge is contextual and relative.	Student used to think that scientists always had a single right answer, but now finds that each theory can be used effectively in a given situation.

Regarding the first three categories as applied to chemical bonding, Finster has given an example in which he asks us to imagine that a teacher has just finished a traditional lecture on an introduction to Valence Bond Theory and Molecular Orbital Theory, summarizing the advantages and disadvantages of each as applied to the explanation of the properties of the homo nuclear diatomic molecules of Period Two in the Periodic Table. The Perry schema offers a possible framework for understanding the various student responses.

Although Finster recognized that students can be found anywhere along the line of progress within the Perry scheme, the realistic fact is that most freshmen function as dualists and that general chemistry classes are largely filled with dualistic thinkers who expect a dualistic approach. However, it is appropriate to promote growth along the scheme using the strategy of developmental instruction. Finster has suggested, in a matrix of challenge and support issues for general chemistry classes, ways in which dualists, multiplists, and relativists can be both supported and challenged. For example, dualists are supported by a highly structured course that includes lectures providing clearly defined terms, a detailed syllabus, a clear set of expectations, homework assignments that parallel the text material, and so forth. Multiplists can be supported and dualists can be challenged by organizing the course with some flexibility concerning content and sequencing, by providing some directions about how to generate problem solving strategies, by structuring group work and analysis of laboratory results by groups, and by having students control or design some aspects of the learning experience. Relativists can be supported and multiplists can be challenged by providing for a more independent learning environment, by encouraging students to develop their own definition of problems and to work out their own solutions, by letting students select their own laboratory problems and modify the design, by providing an historical/societal context for the course content, and by testing across the whole range of Bloomís taxonomy. Other challenge/support issues are diversity of the learning experience, methods of experiential learning, and personalism. While it is obvious that the Perry schema can be an exciting challenge to the traditional way in which chemical educators have ìdelivered chemistry,î instructors must proceed with some caution since each will find himself or herself in a unique learning context with a unique student body.

Practice

Critical Areas in Chemical Education

Within the context set forth above, I conducted a survey of approximately a dozen nationally recognized chemical educators. They produced the following ìlaundry listî of critical areas that they feel must be addressed by the chemistry education community. Their remarks have been grouped under the five headings of philosophy, methodology, curriculum, laboratory, and assessmentóalthough there is a great deal of overlap among these areas.

Philosophy

- Learning chemistry is a highly personal endeavor that requires the learner to pass judgment on the significance and degree of interest in what is learned.
- Chemistry is the central science that is connected to all other scientific disciplines.
- Learning is a challenge, and learning chemistry is a big challengeóbut worth it.
- Conveying a sense of grandeur: chemistry is one of the supreme accomplishments of the human mind.
- Abstract principles can be related to everyday happenings; abstractions are not understood unless they can be applied.
- Modern chemical theory evolved through development of models that have continually been perfected through experimental observation.

Methodology

- Teaching chemistry is best approached as a process emphasizing critical-thinking skills and problem-solving skills rather than as the accumulation of memorized information, facts, theories, and algorithms.
- Personal attention to students is very important.
- Meeting students at their level is essential to communication.
- Strategies to cope with verbal and mathematical illiteracy must be devised in cooperation with other campus departments.
- Varied approaches to problem solving help students with varied backgrounds: drill and practice; cultivation of higher order thinking skills; dimensional analysis.
- A discovery, or guided inquiry, format is often a successful approach.
- Variations on lecture, such as cooperative learning, demonstrations, experimentation, small group discussions, and so forth are essential in optimizing the learning process.
- Emphasis on vocabulary building is very important. Learning chemistry is like learning a new language; time must be taken to learn the language of chemistry in association with direct chemistry experiences so that it can serve as a tool for critical thinking.
- Avoidance of lecture entirely is an approach advocated by many chemistry educators. A studentís attention span in lecture is about ten minutes; passive learning amounts to virtually no learning. As an old Chinese proverb says ìTell me, and I will forget; show me, and I may remember, involve me, and I will understand.î

Curriculum

The curriculum should be rational and reasonable. It should not be designed to ìcoverî all aspects of chemistry superficially but should be more depth oriented in its approach.

- Many recognized chemistry educators constantly search for creative alternative ways to introduce students to chemistry.
- It is important to include the social and historical framework in which chemistry is an evolving discipline rather than a static body of knowledge, so that chemistry can be perceived as a human endeavour evolving within a social and political context with all the strengths and fallibilities attendant on human beings.
- Spiralingóthat is, returning to topics periodically at more and more sophisticated levelsóis preferable to broad, superficial coverage of topics.
- Integration of new technology into teaching is essential. Chemistry is ìdoneî using technology, and many areas of chemistry can be better taught using technology.
- Inclusion of the environment as a wellspring from which many chemical examples can be drawn helps to relate the subject matter to the world in which we live.

Laboratory

- A balance of small-scale and macro scale approaches in the laboratory can give the student a broad range of experience with a variety of techniques.
- Emphasis on open-ended procedures and investigative techniques is the hallmark of the constructivist approach in the laboratory.
- It is important to have a balanced approach to safety in the handling of chemicals and apparatus without

prescribing so many caveats that the laboratory process is impeded or halted altogether.

- The laboratory is the place where students have the greatest opportunity to really understand what chemists actually do and how they think.
- Problems of budget, safety, and time should be carefully thought out and addressed; they need not impede laboratory instruction if the laboratory is well planned.

Assessment

- There is need for thoughtful, creative design for assessment instruments.
- Balance in assessing learning is important. Assessment can be overdone by spending excessive time on it; it can be underdone by assessing only very low level skills and knowledge.
- Instructors should include meaningful assessment of laboratory work if they truly believe that it is an essential part of learning and teaching chemistry.

Conclusion Remarks

Whether chemistry educators are involved in teaching introductory courses or more advanced courses, the only thing of which they can be certain is that everything is in a state of flux and is subject to change. Groups of chemistry educators are constantly examining the philosophical underpinnings, assumptions, prerequisites, requirements, and curricula at every level of undergraduate chemistry courses. Such challenges and changes to the status quo are reflected in the contents of the internationally recognized standardized chemistry tests produced by the Examinations Institute of the Division of Chemical Education, ACS. For example, the ACS General Chemistry Examination was once described as presenting chemistry as a collection of facts and equations along dualistic lines:

completely objective; dealing with facts, principles, and equations in a multiple-choice format; excluding issues of value, history, and process and as such a reflection of what chemical educators value. However, things are changing. The ACS Examinations Institute is now exploring ways to ìbreak the bubbleî (of the multiple-choice answer sheet) by designing machine-scored examinations-with more than one correct answeróthat challenge students to think in more multiplistic and relativistic terms. A symposium that addresses these new thoughts in testing and evaluation took place at the Twelfth Biennial Conference on Chemical Education in August, 1992.

It is clear that many thoughtful and concerned chemistry educators are working to optimize chemistry classroom/laboratory instruction nationwide. In interviews with many of these educators, it has also become clear that they also realize that it is imperative to treat chemistry instruction in more than one human dimension. The holistic approach to education no longer allows either student or teacher the security of conventional pedagogy, nor does it allow teacher or learner to become manipulators of knowledge while leaving the inner self unexamined. Scientific principles cannot be divorced from the fundamental ethical principles that guide the decisions that necessarily evolve from scientific research.

❒❒❒

3

Galvanism and Voltaism: Process and Mechanism

Introduction

The first machine for obtaining static electricity, in which a globe of glass was rotated with friction against the hand, had been built by C.A. Hausen. This was a considerable improvement over Otto von Guerickeís apparatus in which the globe was of sulfur. The Swiss physicist, Martin von Planta, replaced the globe by a glass plate and the hand by pieces of leather. The Leyden jar, invented by E. J. von Kleist in Cammin, Prussia, was a small water bottle held in the hand, while an electric charge was applied to a nail stuck into the bottle. It was improved and became widely known through the experiment of J. J. Von Musschenbroek in Leyden, Holland.

Benjamin Franklin adhered to the theory that there is only one electric fluid, whereas those who started from experiments with magnetism mostly preferred to assume two electric fluids. Charles FranÁois de Gisternay Dufay called them the ìvitreousî and the ìresinousî fluids, corresponding to the well-known opposite charges produced by rubbing glass or resin. By means of the torsion balance, a light horizontal metal bar held at its middle by a long fine wire, Charles Augustin Coulomb defined a quantity of electricity which attracts or repulses another quantity in proportion to these quantities and inversely proportional to the square of their distance.

Electricity thus appeared to follow the law which Newton had found for gravitational attraction. Chemical actions of electric sparks were explained as due to the light accompanying the discharge. In 1786 an incident occurred which itself acted like a spark and which initiated an increasingly widening series of investigations. Luigi Galvani (1737-1798), professor of surgical and anatomical operations in Bologna from 1763, had dissected and prepared a frog. It lay on a table on which an electrical machine was being operated by one of his assistants. Suddenly someone observed that the frog began to twitch when the assistant touched it with a scalpel held in his hand. Although this had been observed before, it was a surprise to Galvani. Immediately he began to investigate what had happened. The accident became as fruitful as the earlier one when acid dripped over a tin frame into a dyestuff solution or as the use of a contaminated potash.

Metals are ìconductors of electricity,î a term which Des Aguliers had introduced in 1740. When a non conducting material was used instead of the metallic scalpel, the frogís leg did not twitch when sparks were drawn from the machine. An apparently nebulous idea, that the open air contains electricity while that in the room does not, caused Galvani to suspend the prepared frog from a hook on his garden fence. He observed that the twitching occurred only when the hook, which was in contact with the lumbar nerve, was of a metal different from the iron of the fence, and when the muscle touched the iron. The best result was obtained when one of the metals was silver, the other iron. This seemed to Galvani to present a perfect analogy to a Leyden jar, with the nerve-muscle system as the source of electricity.

Soon after Galvani published his work, Alessandro Volta (1745-1827), professor of physics in Pavia, rejected its basic results. The animal is only an indicator, an electroscope, not the generator of electricity. Replacing the frog leg by a metallic electroscope in which two pieces of thin gold foil are spread apart when electrically charged, Volta demonstrated that thc contact of different metals is sufficient to produce electricity. In 1775, repeating some earlier attempts, Volta constructed an electrophorus, essentially a plate cast from resin, in which electricity is produced by striking with a fox tail. This static electricity induced a charge in a metal plate on which the resin rested. Galvaniís new experiences and Voltaís explanations led from the old electrophorus to the construction of the electrical pile by which Volta thought to imitate natureís means for creating electricity. Volta wrote in a letter to Sir Joseph Banks, March 20, 1800: ìThis apparatus which resembles in form more the natural electrical organ of the electric eel than the Leyden jar and the known electrical batteries, I should like to call it Artificial Electrical Organ.î

FranÁois Arago described this ìorganî (in his eulogy of Volta 1831) as follows: ìIn the beginning of the year 1800 the illustrious professor conceived the idea of forming a long column by piling up, in succession, a disc of copper, a disc of zinc, and a disc of wet cloth, with scrupulous attention not to change this order. What could be expected beforehand from such a combination? Well I do not hesitate to say, this apparently inert mass, this bizarre assembly, this pile of so many couples of unequal metals separated by a little liquid is, in the singularity of effect, the most marvelous instrument which men have yet invented, the telescope and the steam engine not excepted.î

Another arrangement for producing electricity according to Volta was to immerse a zinc and a silver plate in a cup filled with salty water. Several such cups are combined, the silver of one cup being connected by wire to the zinc of the next. Then by touching the two end plates, the electric current can be felt. ìThis circulation of electric fluid without end (this perpetual movement) may seem paradoxical, it may not be explainable, but it is, nonetheless, true and real, one grasps it, so to say, by hand.î

Volta was surprised to obtain such a tangible action out of a simple arrangement of two metals and moisture, and the world shared his surprise. What happened in that electric pile seemed to contradict the idea that forces cannot be created without some other change occurring at the same time, the concept of a conservation of force which Lavoisier had again emphasized just a few years before. Voltaic piles were built in many places, the size of metal plates and the number of metal pairs were varied, different alkalies, acids, and salts were dissolved in the water between the metals. The concept of electrical positive and negative charge was generalized. Polarity became a favourite topic of speculation. The original idea of the two contraries was thus returned to philosophy after the experimenting scientists had instilled new meaning into it. The hand with which Volta used to feel the electrical action was soon replaced by chemicals.

Nicholson and Carlisle observed that the electricity from a pile decomposed solutions of salts and acids in water. Hydrogen gas developed at the wire which was connected with the zinc pole, oxygen at the wire leading to the copper or silver of the pile. W. Cruikshank (1745-1800) explained this as the action of galvanic currents and he ascribed to them the property of combining with oxygen or hydrogen, carrying these substances to the wires and unloading them there.

The zinc pole was called negative, the other, e.g., silver, positive. Jons Jakob Berzelius (1779-1848, Stockholm) and Wilhelm Hisinger reported (1803) that combustible gas or salt bases accumulate at the negative pole, oxygen and acids at the positive pole. Four years later, Humphry Davy (1778, Penzance-1821., Geneva) decomposed potash, not in the dilute solutions commonly used in such experiments but in the presence of only a small amount of moisture, just sufficient to help in melting the potash. A large pile, consisting of 250 pairs of metal plates, each 6X4 inches in size, was connected to the platinum dish on which the potash rested, and to a second platinum dish held on the surface of the material. Soon a ìvivid actionî occurred. Globules of metallic appearance, like mercury, appeared, ìsome of which burnt with explosion and bright flame.î He concluded that these mercury-like globules represented the metal base of potash, potassium. In similar experiments he obtained from soda its metal base, sodium.

Davyís chemical education had started when he was an apprentice of Dr. Borlese, in his native Penzance in Cornwall, and later with Dr. Beddoes in Bristol (1797-1800). From early youth he liked to talk and experiment before gatherings. He owed his position at the Royal Institution, founded in 1800 by Count Rumford, to the success of an introductory lecture. It may be justifiable to assume that his study of Lavoisierís work on the so-called conversion of water into earth stimulated Davy to investigate whether the acids and bases observed upon the electrical treatment of water were not due to its impurities. He found (1800) that small amounts of salt are contained in ordinary water. They are the source from which electricity separates the acids and bases. The water, which he prepared by distillation, avoiding contact with glass and air, was not changed by the passage of galvanic current. Thus pure water was made for the first time.

Davy liked the dramatic presentation of chemical experiments. His inclination toward poetry carried him away when he described the effect of nitrous oxide, the ìlaughing gas.î He created in a state of exaltation. Shortly after the spectacular success of his Bakerian lecture, November 19, 1807, in which he demonstrated the new metals which explode on contact with water, his health broke down. He recovered only slowly, probably never completely. After he was knighted he played the role of the nobleman with a too conscious effort which has been interpreted as a weakness of character, whereas it obviously was the strength of his sense of drama and poetry.

Figure 3.1. Davy's Safety Lamp with a platinum wire which continues to glow after the flame of the lamp is extinguished, due to lack of fresh air.

Many problems were submitted to a scientist of such renown. He found the solution for a safe lamp which could be used in mines without causing an explosion of the dangerous gases. He failed, however, when he tried to improve ventilation in the House of Lords. In 1826 he resigned from the presidency of the Royal Society because of another breakdown and sought recovery in vain while traveling in Italy and Switzerland.

A powerful pile was required for the decomposition of the alkalies in order to produce their metallic bases. The question arose whether the dimension of the metal plates or the number of the metal pairs determined the magnitude of action. Ten piles, each of the same size, developed ten times as much hydrogen and oxygen from water solutions as did one pile alone. Berzelius concluded that the quantities of decomposition products were proportional to the quantities of electricity, and that these quantities are the greater, the larger the surface of contact between metal and conducting liquid is in the pile.

The size of the metal plates, therefore, corresponded to the quantity of electricity obtainable from a pile. The number of metal pairs determined the intensity. Davy needed the 250 pairs, and at least 150 to overcome the great affinity which holds potassium and oxygen together in potash. Berzelius was able to carry out the decomposition with a much shorter pile containing only twenty metal pairs when he used mercury at the negative pole. The affinity between mercury and potassium was so great that it reduced the intensity required for the decomposition of potash. The metallic base, or as Berzelius cautiously called it, ìthe radical of potash,î is then obtained, not in the pure state but as a compound with mercury, an amalgam.

This shows, according to Berzelius, the general reason for the electrochemical effect. It counteracts the forces of chemical combination which are themselves of an electrical nature. Each atom has both positive and negative electricity, not in equal quantities but with the prevalence of one or the other. Therefore elements are either positive or negative, according to the kind of electricity which prevails. The opposite electricity cause chemical combination. Attraction is accompanied by heat and light, as in the discharge of electricity by sparks or through wires. The analogy does not reach very far, however. Heat and light are all that remains after an electric discharge; in a chemical compound the elements continue to be held by a force greater than any mechanical force that could be applied in an attempt to separate them. After the electrical difference has disappeared, destroyed by the attraction, its binding effect remains.

Hegel caustically remarked that in this ëtheory all the chemical qualities ìare put aside and sunk in the abstraction of electricity. How can anybody reproach philosophy for abstracting from specificity and creating empty generalities when it is permitted to forget all the qualities of substantiality because of positive and negative electricity!î

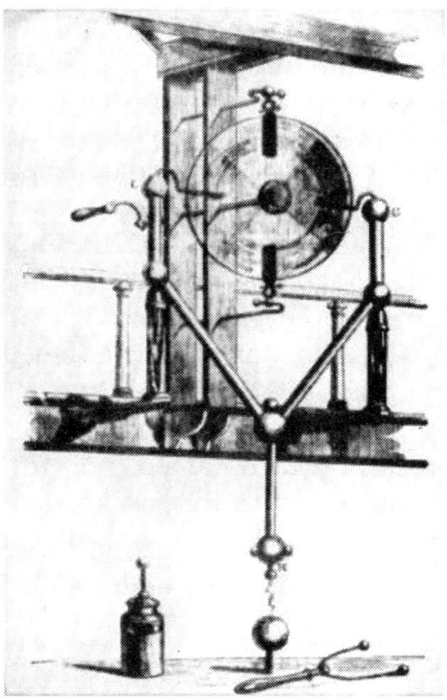

Figure 3.2. Dr, Hare's Electrical Machine. From Robert Hare: "Description of an Electrical Machine".

Berzelius used the assumption of opposite electricities in the atoms ìfor systematic purposes. Since it fitted these purposes exceedingly well, this physically nonsensical theory remained dominant for many years and finally collapsed, not because of its physical, but for its systematic weakness.î Essential parts of the theory were based on the concepts which John Dalton had developed in his theory of the atoms.

In the explanation which William Cruikshank gave for the electrically produced development of oxygen and hydrogen, electricity was a chemical substance. Berzelius, and to some extent also Davy, reversed this explanation and said that chemical substances are electric. One of the contributions to this reversal was Paul Louis Simonís proof that the weight of hydrogen and oxygen produced was equal to the weight of the water lost in the decomposition, so that there was no room for an ìelectric fluidî entering with any weight or substance into this reaction. Another confirmation of the reversed theory was discovered by Davy. When acid, placed in a silver spoon, was neutralized by a stick of caustic soda held in metal pincers while the metals were each connected by wires to the poles of a galvanometer, it indicated an electric charge. The formation of a salt generates electricity. The reversal of the process was thus complete, comprising both the chemical change and the force which accompanies it. On the strength of such findings, affinity was completely identified with electricity, the more easily so because an essential identity of electricity with heat and light was dimly felt to exist.

4

Guidelines for Course Reconfiguration in Chemistry

Introduction

Too often instructors approach teaching on television just as they approach teaching in their traditional classrooms. Last minute preparations, emphasis on verbal rather than visual explanations, lack of handouts, minimally varied instructional strategies, and unpracticed and unenthusiastic presentations are the rule rather than the exception in their teaching style. These instructors have been told frequently by uninformed administrators that teaching on television is the same as traditional teaching. They were told not to change anything and to teach in the way they have always taught. When instructors new to television teaching explore the possible differences in their teaching approaches, they indicate that they would not teach the same way when

- they are physically separated from their students,

- they cannot see their students and receive visual feedback,
- handouts are required rather than optional,
- the unseen students are reluctant to ask questions,
- they teach to a television lens without students present,
- to the second timing is critical,
- involving students at field sites is mandatory,
- videotaping of classes is frequently done for later review by students,
- they donít know who is watching their class.

Planning and organizing a television course will require special provisions, including graphics and visuals in the television format of three units by four units; development of study guides that correspond with the graphics on the television screen; and activities at field sites that involve students in critical thinking. These activities may be conducted at multiple field sites. In addition to these concerns instructors must consider the skills needed for field-site coordinators: the design of a detailed telecourse syllabus; test and examination security; and consumer assessment of the total telecourse. Proper instructor training and practice will eliminate this Achillesí heel of television teaching.

Projecting a Positive Image on Television

Projecting a positive image refers to how the instruction *looks, sounds,* and *moves* on television. It does not mean that the instructor must be tall, dark, handsome or beautiful. When the instructor is well organized he or she projects a positive image of someone who is in charge and excited about what he or she is teaching. Enthusiastic and excited teachers in command of their subject project a positive image because of the energy that they exude.

This energy is contagious and affects most students. Too many television teaching instructors are overly critical of their personal image. They need to look for their positive attributes rather than overemphasize their negative ones. Instructors can videotape themselves for two or three minutes and then critique themselves. By retaping five or six times they can build on their positive attributes. Instructors should determine what type of image they want to project to their television students and take actions that will reinforce this image.

Selecting and Constructing Student Handouts

For many years television students have complained about the lack of coordinated handouts. Handouts minimize student note copying and focus attention on the most important ideas. Handouts also help instructors to organize and sequence their thoughts.

There are a number of techniques available for instructors to develop handouts. These techniques range from broad or detailed outlines to verbatim scripts or a lecture. One technique is called the Interactive Study Guide (ISG). The ISG is a highly organized set of notes, graphics, pictures, charts, and instructional activities. It is used by students during a television lesson or as an accompaniment to a self-directing prepackaged videotape course. Key words, phrases, and other visual materials are printed in logical, numbered segments called ìdisplays.î There are usually two or three displays per page, but a single display could cover two or three pages if necessary. Displays can contain word pictures, activities, short readings, case studies, or directions to complete activities after class (such as a visit to a museum).

Presenting the Subject Matter Verbally and Non-verbally

Although television is a visual medium, oral presentation skills are very important. An instructor can use the best visuals and graphics to make or reinforce a point; but unless that point is heard and understood, it will be lost. Monotone speaking on television will sabotage your lesson. Practice on camera with feedback and constructive criticism from family and colleagues.

Pacing your presentation will help you to emphasize key points and ideas. New material should be introduced at a slower pace than material already covered in class.

Nonverbal communication may be one of the most critical areas that television instructors will need to practice. The whole body can be used to cue, reinforce, show pleasure and displeasure, encourage, and create energy.

Packaging a Self-contained Course on Videotape

A packaged television course is totally self-directing, self-contained, self pacing, and self-correcting. It is designed to be taken for self-study off-campus by individuals or small groups of students. These students can work under supervision or independently. All students take the same final examination.

Visualizing a Television Course

Television is a visual medium. Instructors will have to learn to communicate visually for effective television teaching. All graphics must conform to the television standard three units high by four units wide, which is the way that the television lens sees everything.

One technique that can be used to visualize ideas is called ìword pictures,î which are graphic representations of ideas, concepts, principles, data, and numbers. ìWord picturesî use simple line art, geometric shapes, clip art, symbols, arrows, underlining, textual clues, and color to show relationships among concepts and variables. Designed primarily for information transfer, ìword picturesî are often produced with blank lines, requiring the student to fill in the missing words and phrases. ìWord picturesî usually require a verbal explanation.

Involving Students at Field Sites

Involvement is one of the primary teaching strategies that distinguishes instructional television from educational and commercial television. There are three types of interaction that will benefit students in television courses. These include interactions between the instructor and an individual student that can be heard by all students, interactions among students at an individual field site and among students at different fieldsites, and interactions between a student and the media (as in computer-assisted instruction). At least 50 percent of student time at field-sites should be involved in their own learning.

Incorporating and Responding to Consumer Assessment

Since telecourses are developed for delivery off the main campus, consumer groups purchasing or leasing them will evaluate them in these areas: (1) telecourse organization for television delivery; (2) course logistics, registration, admissions, and student services; (3) appropriate and timely content; (4) technical quality of the audio and video; (5) types and amount of student involvement; (6) quality of handouts; and (7) satisfaction with the teaching.

The perceptions of the consumers as to how well these criteria were met in existing courses will determine their continued support of the telecourses.

Reconfiguration Guidelines to Modify Traditional Courses

Reconfiguration guidelines were derived from the eight areas of teaching that distinguish television teaching from traditional teaching. They are used by an instructor before modifying a course, while modifying a course, and after a course has been modified in order to make all necessary adjustments for presentation on television. Most of these criteria can also apply to audio conferencing, video conferencing, and audio graphic presentations.

❑❑❑

5

Teaching Methodology for Chemistry

Introduction

Recent research indicates that interest in team teaching, faculty collaboration, and interdisciplinary education is increasing. Still, the barriers to collaboration am often substantial. Most aspects of the prevailing culture are built around a model of the teacher as an isolated individual. These notions are reinforced in the culture of the classroom. At the same time, there is widespread recognition that we need to cultivate the ability to work together in both the academy and the workplace, and there is increasing interest in approaches that amplify energy and learning by bringing people together. Team teaching is one strategy for achieving this, but it is pursued for a variety of different purposes and takes many shapes and forms.

Challenges and Opportunities in Team Teaching

Colleges and individual faculty members embrace team teaching for many different reasons. The rationale may be grounded in curricular and student needs, or it may be more faculty centered. Team teaching and interdisciplinary study are often pursued to create a greater sense of academic community and engagement and to build greater curricular coherence for students. Advocates argue that students need explicit structures for academic and social engagement, especially on commuter campuses. From a student perspective, many colleges and universities are experienced as socially and intellectually fragmented environments. Team teaching and interdisciplinary study can provide a holistic counterpoint by bringing multiple disciplinary perspectives together to understand complex issues. As one student put it:

> Evergreen is the first place where I had the opportunity to integrate the bits and chunks of information and to synthesize them into a new understanding of the world where I live, of myself, and of my role as a member of society. It's like the difference between collecting a pile of bricks and building a house.

Team teaching and interdisciplinary education also makes sense to those who believe that diverse, multidisciplinary perspectives are necessary for understanding the complexities of the modern world. In response to this need, over the past twenty years many new cross disciplinary majors and areas of study have developed, including environmental studies, ethnic studies, and cognitive science, to mention just a few. These constitute fertile territory for team teaching.

Team teaching also addresses faculty-development needs. Teaching the same courses year after year can be a lonely, repetitive, and fragmented experience. Team teaching can provide faculty members with a new perspective on their students, their colleagues, and teaching in general. Many faculty members find that team teaching helps them clarify their goals. As one faculty member put it, ìTeaching in front of other instructors helped me look at myself the way the students look at me. It made me think much more clearly about what I wanted to accomplish in terms of learning outcomes.î Other faculty members see team teaching as a way to learn new approaches. As one remarked: ìIím interested in broadening my teaching techniquesóseeing how others do it, learning from them and applying what I see to be helpful to my own classes.î Team teaching can provide confidence to try new approaches and experiment with new ways of involving students, such as working in groups or using writing across the curriculum.

When two teachers from different disciplines team up, they gain new insights into their disciplines. As one teacher observed, When you am in the room with a person in another discipline, you become curious about the way things are seen by a person not of your discipline, or the way a concept is used that is so fundamental to what you do, that you take it for granted. You get asked wonderful questions, and you ask more questions. This brings you to entirely new frames. You reveal yourself in a whole new way. This simply doesnít happen when you teach solo.

Another faculty member remarked that team teaching gave him a much clearer perspective on the differences between disciplines:

> I'm coming to understand the strengths and perspectives unique to each field. When I lecture I'm comfortable with sweeping themes, categories, and timelines to explain the flow of history in our seminars I am impressed with my colleagues' use of literary analysis, poetic devices, and other perspectives that pass me by. We are all realizing the strengths we bring to our teaching as we are introduced to new ways to deal with the same content.

Team teaching can also build collegial relationships and foster respect. As one of the twenty-year veterans remarked:

> While team teaching provided many other ways of looking at the subjects I teach, it also taught me to recognize the value of colleagues who I'd only previously known as we passed in the hall or sat next to in a dismal faculty meeting. These are changes that are useful. Changes come from the tension between various

> ways of looking at a problem, and this comes inevitably from working together.

While team teaching is often justified solely on the grounds of offering a creative venue for faculty members, it is also done for more specific strategic reasons. It might be used to mentor senior and junior faculty, to build relations between skill and content courses, or to bring related educational services (such as the library or student affairs) into the classroom. At one college, team teaching was integral to developing a more multicultural curriculum. As an economist, who was team teaching in a program on South Africa, Ireland, and Palestine, noted:

> The interdisciplinary program "Problems without Solutions?" provided an invaluable yearlong multicultural learning experience for both the students and the faculty. It provided a way for faculty to learn new content as well as new pedagogical approaches. Each member of the team had something to contribute: no single individual could have ever taught this program alone.

Team teaching helps model diversity by bringing multiple perspectives into the classroom. Many faculty members say they enjoy team teaching because it is inevitably more creative; the synergy that can come from multiple points of view can be remarkable. It is of special benefit in interdisciplinary areas and in building bridges between skill courses and ìcontent classes.î It can give teachers in repetitve skill classes a stronger platform from which to teach by placing the skill classes in a disciplinary context, and it certainly deepens studentsí analytic abilities when writing is made an integral part of the course. Both students and faculty find team-taught classes highly stimulating environments. They often have a quality of energy and excitement, a kind of contagious enthusiasm, which is exciting.

Forms of Team Teaching

Team teaching comes in many different shapes and forms. Some approaches dramatically alter conventional ways of defining curriculum and faculty roles and relationships, while others barely disturb traditional ways of operating. Depending upon the form it takes, team teaching will raise different issues.

Team teaching can take place within a single discipline when several teachers collaborate, or it can involve collaboration among different disciplines. Some forms of team teaching leave the disciplinary content basically in place while others transform it. Team teaching also varies regarding faculty roles and relationships. In some variants, there is a clear differentiation of roles and a hierarchy; in others, the roles are nearly interchangeable. Some forms of team teaching cast faculty members in the role of generalists while others are built around their expertise as specialists. Team-teaching approaches also vary as far as faculty interdependence is concerned. Some approaches involve relatively little interdependence and coplanning; in others the collaboration is thoroughgoing and includes virtually all aspects of planning and delivering the course. Which approach is most appropriate and viable depends upon the institutional environment and the goals behind team teaching.

Team teaching can take a variety of different forms, and the notion of who is even appropriate to include in a faculty team varies considerably. Probably the most basic question to clarify is why team teaching is being undertaken and which approaches are most viable.

Issues of Viability

To flourish, team teaching must be viable from the standpoint of the students, the faculty, and the institution. Yet, in fact few institutions provide a truly hospitable environment for team teaching, and many aspects of the existing ways of doing things get in the way. Nonetheless, them are some promising exceptions, and creative ways of addressing some recurrent concerns are being found, even in institutions that make only limited commitments to collaborative teaching.

Cost

Cost is the most frequently cited barrier to team teaching. It is often contended that team teaching is inherently inefficient because it produces fewer student credit hours per instructor, particularly when compared with large lecture classes. As one faculty member put it: ìThe administration said they supported team teaching, but when it got right down to it we only got half credit for teaching the class together. Our colleagues thought we were fools for doing it at all, but we really enjoyed it. Still, we couldnít sustain teaching a double load for more than one quarter. We felt exploited.î Hundreds of faculty members who have attempted and then abandoned team teaching for this reason would echo this complaint.

While many forms of team teaching are not as cost effective as large lecture classes, their viability depends largely upon how they are designed and how cost effectiveness is measured. Some forms of team teaching try to produce both the efficiency of lectures and the intimacy of smaller classes. For example, one team-teaching model involves a core set of plenary lectures for large numbers of students accompanied by smaller discussion classes.

Learning Communities

Learning communities and course clustering models also produce more viable approaches to team teaching. ìLearning communitiesî are curricular restructuring approaches that reconfigure courses into larger clusters to produce more curricular coherence and opportunities for active learning and more interaction between students and faculty. By combining courses into larger units of credit, learning communities often produce student-faculty ratios roughly equivalent to conventional notions of faculty load.

In Washington (USA) state a variety cf different learning-community approaches are being used. These range from linked courses in which a cohort of students co-register to more thoroughly integrated clusters of three or even four courses. A four-credit class with twenty students will never support two faculty members at most colleges; as a result, each teacher is often given only a half-course credit for team teaching such a course. This solution does not respect the fact that two instructors are, in fact, teaching the class. Team teaching is thereby penalized and the long-run viability of the enterprise depends upon faculty voluntarism. If, on the other hand, a team-taught class is offered for eight credits with forty students, it will more adequately support two faculty members. Many colleges are finding that large numbers of team-taught, linked courses can be offered through this approach.

Two other comments are in order in thinking about issues of cost effectiveness. First, itís important to recognize that all colleges have an internal political economy in the distribution of student credit hours and faculty load. Some courses always subsidize others. In most institutions, large freshman classes subsidize upper-division courses as well as faculty release time to do research. The important question is where the subsidies should be lodged. For example, an argument can be made that ìfrontloadingî the curriculum with smaller classes in the freshman year would be more cost effective as far as student retention is concerned since so many students are lost in the first year of college.

Second, team-taught courses may or may not be worth subsidizing depending on oneís notion of ìefficiency.î Certainly some models are more costly than others, but ultimately this question of efficiency can only be addressed by thinking through both the costs and benefits as well as the opportunity costs in a given institutional environment. In doing this analysis, itís important to consider what we mean by being ìefficient.î A complex and demanding calculus of educational efficiency would look at student learning, retention, and faculty vitality rather than simply the numbers of students in a class. Eight years of research in the state of Washington suggest that team-taught, course-clustering approaches have high payoff as far as ìeducational efficiencyî is concerned, as measured by student retention, student motivation, student achievement, and faculty renewal but funding models remain an obstacle in allocating resources because student enrollment remains the principal yardstick.

Quality

Some question the quality of team teaching, arguing that it produces a less coherent curriculum and that it is often disorganized. At one university, for example, a team of five to nine faculty members ìteam taughtî an introductory course in architecture that provided an overview of the field. Each member of the faculty team presented his or her specialty. This rotational form of team teaching could perhaps be better described as ìtake-turnî teaching. When it became apparent that there was virtually no coordination and communication between the faculty, students complained. The net result was that students experienced a poorly organized curriculum, lack of clear expectations, and numerous unproductive gaps and redundancies in the reading, the presentations, and the assignments. Poorly organized efforts give team teaching a bad reputation.

Quality concerns may also be about whether team-taught courses ìmeasure upî as far as specific educational outcomes and content coverage is concerned. The implication is that team-taught classes, particularly interdisciplinary ones, compromise and dilute the content of freestanding courses taught by a single professor. It is certainly a legitimate empirical question to ask how a team taught interdisciplinary course combining American history and American literature compares with separate courses. Similarly, we need to ask which approaches are best for building skills: how do freestanding composition courses compare with writing across the curriculum approaches that embed writing in a discipline?

Unfortunately, we have little empirical data to assess how team-taught classes compare with courses taught by a single teacher. Here again Washington state provides the most comprehensive information available (assessment of the learning-community effort has been ongoing since 1984 in more than two dozen colleges and universities). But the Washington data does not directly answer this question since the learning-community effort alters a variety of characteristics in the teaching and learning environment in addition to team teaching. Klein and Austin and Baldwin have provided additional recent information on faculty collaboration, but the most systemic information about faculty collaboration is in nonteaching settings.

When examined closely, most of the quality concerns about organization, coherence, and coverage are empirical questions or issues about how team taught courses are designed. While team-taught courses can be disorganized and have less focus and coherence, these certainly are not inherent flaws.

Development of Teachers Who Can Team Teach

Team teaching can be a powerful vehicle for faculty members to learn from one another. It breaks open the sanctity of the classroom and provides opportunities for day-to-day observation, coaching, and faculty development. As higher education enters a critical transition point with many faculty retirements, team teaching has special value in building the dialogue between generations. It can provide an invaluable vehicle for senior faculty members to mentor those just entering the academy while also reinvigorating senior faculty with the energy and fresh perspectives of their more recently educated colleagues.

At the same time, team teaching can be challenging. It goes against the grain of most teacherís prior training and experience. Most of us have no role models and few opportunities for acquiring the skills of collaborative teaching. The more intense forms of team teaching require flexibility, the ability to ìshare the stageî and negotiate content and pedagogy, and genuine curiosity about other perspectives. Team teaching often works best when teachers have a clear sense of their own authority and a willingness to meet others at the boundaries of their fields. Some disciplinary combinations may work better than others. Jerry Gaff and Robert Wilsonís early research on faculty cultures in different disciplines showed marked differences between the pedagogical styles and strategies of faculty members in different fields. Kleinís recent summary of research on teamwork has also indicated the importance of other variables, such as status, tenure, and size of teams. The work of Gabelnick suggests that women and teachers in the humanities are drawn disproportionately to learning-community teaching. Working closely with colleagues requires a considerable investment of time and energy to think through and plan a course together. For those who truly enjoy collaborative teaching, the intense intellectual energy and collegiality that comes from this ìextra timeî is part of the reward. For others, accustomed to a more contained process of planning, the investment might be harder to make. Many admit that comfort with team teaching comes gradually. Thinking about her initial experience, an English teacher remarked: ìIt was an almost painful experience, to break old habits, to think in new ways. I had become very confident and set in the way I presented my courses. Teaching with two others required rethinking what we were teaching, how we were teaching, what was really essential. At firs, the whole thing derailed me pedagogically. I was really anxious!î

Creating Structure to Support Team Teaching

Used on any scale, team teaching has broad implications for faculty hiring, training, and evaluation. To flourish, it must be valued in an institutionís reward system. At Evergreen State College in America, for example, interest in collaborative learning and teaching is one of the criteria used for hiring and evaluating faculty, and peer review is a cornerstone of the faculty reappointment system. Many other colleges in Washington state, which is the site of the largest statewide effort around team teaching, are also specifically seeking faculty members with interest and skill in collaborative teaching.

Colleges genuinely committed to team teaching need to find ways to support it. This requires creating a climate that encourages risk taking, supports innovation, and provides opportunities to build faculty skills in collaborative teaching. At Evergreen State College a number of new ìdialogue formsî have evolved to support faculty collaboration. Faculty seminars are an important cornerstone. All faculty teams are required to hold these weekly meetings, which provide a forum for the team to share their different perspectives on the major text of the week. The seminar is often a critical barometer of how well a team is functioning. In addition, all teams write a faculty covenant outlining each personís roles and responsibilities and their common understandings. The covenant is often less important as a document than it is as a process of publicly stating and negotiating expectations. As one Evergreen veteran put it, ìThe only situation worse than a team having to enforce its covenant is a team which does not have a covenant to enforceî.

Other methods of supporting collaboration have evolved elsewhere. Seattle Central Community College holds annual debriefings where faculty teams meet to share their experiences. Tacoma Community College and Spokane Falls Community College provide ways for faculty interested in team teaching to literally ìkibitzî on the process in advance by observing another team the quarter before they start team teaching.

It provides various activities including faculty exchanges, print resources, conferences, technical assistance, and annual curriculum planning retreats for faculty teams to come together and plan their curriculum with assistance from more experienced hands. Faculty exchanges have proved to be a particularly effective vehicle for beginners to learn from those with more experience in team teaching.

Summary

There is currently considerable debate about the quality of higher education, and many believe that greater attention needs to be paid to teaching. This debate comes at a critical time when a large proportion of the nationís faculty will retire and be replaced. The prognosis for a renewed emphasis on teaching is decidedly mixed. Most predict that the 1990s will be a period of financial austerity with few resources for large-scale innovation. Many of the nationís graduate schools are producing scholars who are increasingly specialized and devoted primarily to research. At the same time, public attention is clearly shifting towards greater educational performance and more emphasis on teaching. Much creative thinking is now focused on how to revitalize faculty, improve student learning, evaluate and reward teaching, and bridge the gap between scholarship and teaching.

We think a renewed emphasis on team teaching is especially timely now. Team teaching is an excellent vehicle for building bridges between an increasingly segmented faculty. It is a natural way of bringing new scholarship into the classroom in such areas as ethnic studies and womenís studies. Through collaborative teaching new pedagogical approaches can be introduced with day-to-day opportunities for observation and learning. Team teaching can produce a multiplier effect for innovation in a variety of areas. It provides a natural avenue for strengthening student abilities by bridging skills and content interfaces in the curriculum. In the 1960s and 1970s there was considerable interest in team teaching, but many of the models were not viable. The renaissance of interest in team teaching in the 1990s is more sophisticated, and there are many more cost-effective approaches available.

Team teaching has larger lessons to impart about creating structures for working together, about developing vehicles for ongoing learning, and about respecting and modeling diversity. As Peter Senge has pointed out in his provocative book *The Fifth Discipline*: ìWe can build learning organizations, organizations where people continually expand their capacities where new and expansive forms of thinking are nurtured, where collective aspiration is set free, and where people are continually learning how to learn together.î At this critical time of transition in the academy, team teaching is one avenue for opening up the learning process and for building a greater sense of community in our institutions.

❑❑❑

6

Encouraging Student for Team Work

Introduction

We devised a very quick and simple measure: we simply asked students to indicate what was the single main reason why they were studying at university. The responses were, of course, many and varied, but we were able to categorize the great majority of them into three main categories, which we called ëstop gapí, ëmeans to an endí and ëpersonal developmentí. The percentage figures give the proportion of students who were placed into each category out of a university sample of 844 students whose responses could be categorized.

Those classified as stop-gap students (10 per cent) were studying because they could think of nothing else to do, wanted to defer taking a decision, or simply wanted to enjoy themselves for three years. Those classed as means-to-an-end students wanted to achieve something through their degree, whether this was a better paid or more interesting job, or simply qualifications to put after their names. This was much the most common category, with two-thirds of our sample being classified in this way. Personal development students (nearly a quarter of our sample) were ones who were interested in the subject itself or wanted to use their degree to realize their own potential or to develop their personal skills.

While the classification was largely *post hoc,* and was carried out with incomplete knowledge of existing educational theories of motivation, it is striking how similar our classification is to those arrived at by other researchers. For example, a key distinction is often made between intrinsic and extrinsic motivation. Intrinsically motivated students enjoy a challenge, want to master the subject, are curious and want to learn; while extrinsically motivated students are concerned with the grades they get, external rewards and whether they will gain approval from others. While the fit is not perfect, the parallels with our own classification system are clear, with intrinsic motivation corresponding closely to personal development and extrinsic motivation corresponding to means to an end.

Other major distinctions that have been made in the literature also map closely onto our categorization. Dweck and Elliott have drawn the highly influential distinction between performance goals and learning goals. Students with performance goals are motivated primarily by obtaining good marks, while learning oriented students wish to actually learn something from their studies.

Performance goals are linked to means to an end (and extrinsic motivation), while learning goals are linked with personal development (and intrinsic motivation). Other distinctions in the literature related to Dweckís are those between ability and mastery goals and between ego involvement and task involvement. There are, of course, important differences in emphasis in all these approaches, but there is enough similarity between them, and enough overlap with the distinctions made in our own characterization, to conclude that the concepts underlying them are reasonably consistent and widespread.

Interrogating Practice

What do you know about the motivation of the students you teach? If they are training for a specific career, does this affect their motivation in a particular way?

A Motivation and Achievement of Motivation

Stop-gap motivation was not especially common in our student sample, but it did occur. While this has not been extensively discussed in the literature, the related concept of amotivation has received some attention. Deci and Ryan describe amotivated students as ones who do not really know why they are at university, think themselves incompetent and feel that they have little control over what happens to them. In a real sense, then, these students show an absence of motivation.

This highlights another aspect of motivation: that it has strength as well as direction. Thus far we have looked at motivational goals, in other words what studentsí aims are. But even students with identical goals may have very differing strengths of that motivation. A simple example would be two students, both of whom were studying to get a better job, for one of whom it was their lifelong and heartfelt ambition, and for the other of whom it was little more than a passing interest. Although their motives would be the same, the different strengths of these motives might be expected to lead to very different behavioural outcomes, for example in their ability to persevere in adversity.

Many educational writers discuss achievement motivation as one of the principal factors influencing outcomes in higher education. A student who is high in achievement motivation can be seen as lying at the opposite end of the scale from an amotivated student. The former student is concerned primarily with achieving a successful outcome at the end of his or her studies. This cuts across many of the dimensions discussed earlier, in that both extrinsically and intrinsically motivated students can be high or low in achievement motivation. In other words, achievement motivation is largely a measure of the strength of motivation, rather than of its direction.

It is a gross over-simplification, but nevertheless it seems reasonable to suggest that our own research and the existing literature have identified three main types of motivation: intrinsic, extrinsic and achievement motivation (with amotivation simply being the opposite end of the continuum to achievement motivation). Clearly, however, it is of little use knowing what studentsí motives are unless the impact of these on how students behave is known.

Motives and Behaviour

There is surprisingly little evidence as to the behaviour associated with different motives. Some fairly simplistic predictions can be made. For example, one might expect that students high in achievement motivation will actually achieve higher grades. Furthermore, given that intrinsic motivation seems so central to higher education, one would surely expect that students with this motivation should perform better academically than those with extrinsic motivation. One might also predict that the study strategies would be different in different groups of students; for example, intrinsically motivated students might be expected to develop a deeper understanding of the material than extrinsically motivated ones, and perhaps also to be more resistant to discouragement in the light of a poor mark. There is, surprisingly, little clear-cut evidence on any of these predictions.

One line of evidence concerning the relationship between motives and behaviour derives from the work on studentsí approaches to studying. Research into these approaches, using the approaches to studying inventory, is arguably the most extensively researched area in higher education in recent years. The main focus of this research has been on the distinction between deep and surface approaches to studying. A deep approach is concerned with conceptual understanding of the material, and incorporating this into oneís existing knowledge; whereas a surface approach is characterized by rote learning of material, with the intention of reproducing this in another context (e.g., an examination). Each of these approaches is linked to a certain type of motivation, with deep approaches being associated with intrinsic motivation and surface approaches with extrinsic motivation.

Crucially from the present perspective, these associations were derived empirically, through the use of factor analysis. What this means is that specific types of motivation and specific approaches to studying tended to be associated with each other in the responses given by students to questionnaire items. Subsequent research has shown the main factors to be remarkably robust. However, the link between motives and strategies may not be as neat as it seems at first sight. Pintrich and Garcia found that intrinsically motivated students did indeed use strategies designed to develop a conceptual understanding of material, but that extrinsically motivated students did not, as would have been predicted, use more rehearsal strategies.

In addition to deep and surface approaches, another approach consistently emerges in the analysis of responses to the Approaches to Studying Inventory. This is usually termed the strategic approach, and it is closely related to achievement motivation. Strategic students vary their approach depending on the circumstances; if they judge that a surface approach is necessary in one situation, they will use it, but in others they might use a deep approach. Their main aim is to secure high marks and they will adapt their strategy in whatever way they see fit to try to achieve this aim.

Australian research by Biggs has also identified achieving orientation as a major factor in studentsí approaches to learning. Biggs characterizes the achieving motivation as a desire to obtain high grades even when the task to be completed does not inspire interest. Biggs states that this motive is facilitated by competition which provides students with the opportunity to increase their self-esteem.

In the same way as Entwistle and Ramsden, Biggs associates this type of motivation with a specific learning strategy, which he terms the achieving strategy but which is very similar to the strategic approach.

The relationship between motivation and academic success has been investigated by Pintrich and Garcia and the picture that emerges is not a simple one. Overall, there was no direct relationship between intrinsic motivation and academic success, but instead an interaction between motivation and the strategy adopted. In essence, students who lack intrinsic motivation can still perform well, providing they adopt appropriate study strategies to compensate for this. Research into studentsí approaches to studying has produced mixed results. While some authors have reported a correlation between deep approaches and academic success this is not always found to be the case. Hence there is little evidence to support the claim that intrinsic motivation leads to academic success. As we shall see, one possible reason for this is that intrinsic motivation, while valued by lecturers, is not necessarily rewarded in the assessments they give students.

Interrogating Practice

Reflect on the correlation between motivation and academic achievement as demonstrated by students you teach. How well do your intrinsically motivated students perform?

Measuring Student Motivation

In addition to the measures of achievement motivation contained within the instruments developed by Entwistle and Ramsden and Biggs, a small number of other motivation measures has been developed specifically for use with students in higher education. The two most important of these are the Academic Motivation Scale developed by Vallerand and the Motivated Strategies for Learning Questionnaire developed by Pintrich.

The Academic Motivation Scale consists of 28 items which are designed to assess three types of intrinsic motivation, three types of extrinsic motivation, and amotivation. It would appear to have reasonable reliability and validity and its short length means that it can realistically be used in educational research.

The Motivated Strategies for Learning is a much longer scale, containing 81 items, with rather more sub-scales. It is also US-oriented, and thus far seems to have not been used in this country. Although the scale has good reliability and validity, it is rather too long to be of great use in educational research, at least outside the United States.

Development of Motivation

We have seen the kinds of things that motivate students, leading us to consider their motivation through the years of a degree course.

Interrogating Practice

In your experience, do students come to university with high motivation? What happens to their motivation during their stay at university? Does your department inspire them to ever higher levels of motivation? If so, how?

One measure of studentsí motivations on arriving at university is Entwistleís Approaches to Study Skills Inventory for Students (ASSIST). Part of this involves questions about reasons for entering higher education.

These results are broadly consistent with the findings obtained using a very different method (and on students already in higher education) by Newstead, Franklyn-Stokes and Armstead. The main reasons for entering higher education were to get a good job and to develop useful skills (i.e., means to an end). Next most frequent were reasons relating to personal development, such as to study subjects in depth and develop as a person. Less frequent were the stop-gap reasons, such as to delay taking a decision or simply drifting into higher education. The only slight mismatch is in the high ranking given in the Sharpe study to an active social and sporting life. This is probably because the reason is indeed an important one for many people, but is seldom the single most important reason.

The similarity of the findings in these two studies might suggest that studentsí motives do not change a great deal over the course of their degrees. There is direct support for this contention in the research of Fazey. They used Vallerandís Academic Motivation Scale to carry out a longitudinal investigation of studentsí motivation over the first two years of their degree courses at the University of Bangor. Their results indicated that students were high on both intrinsic and extrinsic motivation on entry to university but much lower on amotivation. From the present perspective, the interesting finding was that the levels of these three types of motivation showed virtually no change over the first two years at university. In a sense this is a disappointing finding since one might have hoped that higher education would have led to students becoming more intrinsically motivated by their subject. It is of course possible that this does happen to some students but is offset by an equal number who become less intrinsically motivated. A similar finding emerged in a study by Jacobs and Newstead who found that studentsí interest in their discipline seemed, if anything, to decline over the course of their studies.

Encouraging Student Motivation

Lecturers frequently bemoan the lack of student motivation and ask what they can do to improve this. We hope that the foregoing overview will have at least hinted that there is no quick fix. Indeed, before even addressing this issue it is necessary to ascertain what aspect of student motivation needs to be addressed. Most lecturers would agree that a complete lack of motivation of any kind-amotivation-is highly undesirable. Further, most lecturers would claim that intrinsic motivation is more desirable than extrinsic.

First, then, how can we avoid students becoming amotivated? For some students, this will be next to impossible, since they may have entered higher education with the sole aim of enjoying the social life. But there is also evidence that what we do to students at university can lead to their becoming amotivated. Hoskins has recently completed a research programme investigating studentsí approaches to essay writing, and has discovered through a combination of focus groups and questionnaires that certain factors of this process lead to students losing motivation. Of particular importance is the feedback given, both in terms of the mark awarded and the written feedback provided.

One group of students approached essay writing with an understanding motivation, in that they enjoyed writing, had an intrinsic interest in the essay and tended to read extensively. Because of the amount of reading they did, they often had problems focusing their essay and adhering to the word limit. As a result they tended to receive poor marks but had difficulty in understanding where they had gone wrong or what skills they needed to overcome the problems. These students felt that marking was often inconsistent and contained insufficient detail to be helpful. In consequence, they avoided using an understanding motivation on the grounds that they felt it unlikely to lead to a good mark.

One of the most prominent themes in the focus group data collected by Hoskins was the almost unanimous perception of essay marks as unsatisfactory. Students often felt that there was no relationship between the amount of effort they put into an essay and the mark they were awarded, and that it took a disproportionate amount of effort to achieve small percentage increases. They were highly critical of what they regarded as a ëglass ceilingí-an unwritten rule which seems to prevent them getting marks higher than an upper second. Since they found it relatively easy to produce an essay which got a high lower second or low upper second mark, there was little incentive to do any extra work given the existence of this glass ceiling. The belief that the range of marks awarded for essays is too limited given the potential range available was also a constantly recurring theme.

It is only part of the answer to this problem, but it would appear that one way of avoiding amotivation is to make sure that students are given full and appropriate feedback; and, if it is clear that they have put in extra work and not received a particularly high mark, then feedback on why this has occurred needs to be given. When terms such as ëdeveloping an argumentí are used, there needs to be some explanation of what this means. One way of achieving this might be by setting up a database of examples which could act as an essay feedback bank that staff could draw on. This would enable them to demonstrate what aspects of an essay are likely to attract good marks. The use of marking schemes also has the potential to improve the quality of the feedback, though there is the danger here of ëdownslidingí, where students (and perhaps staff also) focus on low level activities such as correcting spelling mistakes at the expense of more complicated revisions such as trying to develop an argument.

Of course, lecturers will argue that they have insufficient time to do all this, and there is undoubtedly truth in this. What may be required is an overhaul of assessment systems so that lecturers are able to give appropriate feedback. If the assessment process is so overwhelming that proper feedback cannot be given, then there is surely something wrong with the system.

Interrogating Practice

What does your feedback do to your studentís perceptions of their own ability? Does it encourage motivation or amotivation?

The second issue is that of how to encourage intrinsic rather than extrinsic motivation. There is much evidence to suggest that the majority of students tend to adopt surface approaches (of which extrinsic motivation is a part) at university.

Again there is no easy or guaranteed solution to this, and some authors are rather pessimistic as to what can be achieved by individual lecturers or even groups of lecturers. Biggs points out that university education is part of a system, and that most systems are resistant to change, instead tending to return to the state of balance that has developed within them. What this means is that studentsí approaches to study and their motives are determined by a number of aspects of the higher education system, including their perception of the department and university they are in, and even of the university system in general. Trying to change studentsí motives by changing the way one module or group of modules is taught is unlikely to be effective, since all the other aspects will be working against this change. Similar rather disappointing conclusions come from attempts to train students to approach their studies in different ways. Norton and Crowley found that the training programme they devised had little effect on how students studied. Purdie and Hattie found that their training programme led to a temporary improvement in approaches to studying but that these rapidly reverted after the training came to an end.

However, there is one aspect of higher education which does seem to be crucially important in studentsí motivation, and that is the assessment system. Entwistle describe how final year students start with good intentions, are intrinsically motivated and attempt to adopt deep approaches to their studies; however, as examination time approaches they become increasingly extrinsically motivated and adopt surface, rote learning approaches. Similar findings have emerged in research by Newstead and Findlay. One way of changing this might be if the assessment system were to be one which encouraged conceptual understanding as opposed to rote learning. It would appear that the standard three-hour essay-based examination does tend to produce surface approaches, despite the best intentions of lecturers. This might be altered through the increased use of problem solving, case studies and the like, where knowledge has to be used rather than just learnt. What is more, such assessments could take place under formal examination conditions, thus avoiding some of the problems associated with continuous assessment.

Finally, it may be possible to guide students to help themselves by encouraging them to adopt strategies which will keep up their motivation. A recent study by Wolters investigated the kinds of strategies that students used to regulate their own motivation, and found that these varied between students and as a function of the task in question. Among the most common strategies were reminding themselves of the extrinsic rewards (usually the need to do well in an exam), cognitional strategies such as reading through notes and preparing new notes, and changing the environment in which studying was taking place (eg, taking breaks or moving to a quieter room). It is not known which of these strategies were the most effective and it is probably the case that they will not be equally effective for all students, but informing students of the self-regulatory strategies available might conceivably be of some help.

7

Teaching Chemistry in Small Groups

Definition and Meaning

It is viewed as an exciting, challenging and dynamic method open to use in a variety of forms and to serve a range of purposes appropriate to different disciplines. Therefore terms will be explored in their most diverse and flexible forms. The process is identified not as a didactic one but rather as a participative experience, in which students are encouraged to take responsibility, along with tutors, for their own learning. Electronic discussion groups may also promote learning.

A Highly Skilled Activity

Many writers argue that small group teaching is among the most difficult and highly skilled of teaching techniques. In addition to the primary objective of teaching students to think, the tutor must have a number of subsidiary objectives if the small group is to function. Writers generally agree that the method requires a wide knowledge of subject matter and ability to attend to detail while keeping an eye on the overall picture. Appreciation of how groups function, openness of spirit, accommodation of different views, receptivity to new ideas and maturity to manage a group of students without dominating them, are all necessary for effective small group teaching. These attributes are best thought of as skills to be developed over a period of time.

Not only do tutors have to learn how to teach using small group methods but also students have to learn how to work in small groups. Here, it is assumed that it is the tutorís job to assist students to learn, to equip them with self-confidence and facilitate group cohesion. Therefore, a tutor using these methods is much more than a subject matter expert.

In recognizing that small group teaching is a difficult and highly skilled teaching technique, it is important to know that it is also one of the most potentially rewarding teaching and learning methods for tutors and students alike.

Group Size

Small group teaching, broadly speaking, is any teaching and learning occasion which brings together between 2 and 20 participants. The participants may be students and their tutors, or students working on their own. Because of the relatively small numbers of students involved, the financial cost of the method can be high.

Context

In recent years the experience of small group teaching and learning has come under threat. With the expansion of student numbers in higher education, class sizes have increased dramatically; tutored small group teaching is expensive when compared with the lecture. A resulting re-examination has had a profound impact on small group teaching and learning. It has led many tutors to re-evaluate critically the nature of the method and to maximize its potential to the full with some quite interesting and innovative results. Peer tutoring, peer assessment, peer learning and peer support have become more common. In defence of the method, it has been necessary for assurances to be made that time devoted to teaching in this format is well organized and well spent.

This re-examination has also coincided with other changes in the external environment. The implementation of accreditation of university teachers has grown rapidly since the establishment of the Institute for Learning and Teaching in 1999, and is resulting in a considerable culture shift. Part of this shift involves a growing recognition by lecturers that they are responsible not only for what is taught but also, in part, for how students learn.

Learning in Small Groups

The interpersonal and interactive nature of small groups makes them a challenging and appropriate vehicle for engaging students in their own learning. Students are engaged in small groups, both as learners and as collaborators in their own intellectual, personal and professional development. Furthermore, there is strong evidence from students themselves that they benefit from, and enjoy, the experience in a whole range of different ways. These might best be summed up as both cognitive and affective in nature. Alongside understanding and knowledge benefits, students suggest that participation, belonging and being involved are all important dimensions of the experience. The implications of these findings are that the process of building and managing groups, and assisting with the development of relationships, is of paramount importance.

The small group is viewed as a critical mechanism for exploring the development of a range of key skills. It is within the small group that self-confidence can be improved, and teamwork and interpersonal communication developed.

Development of these group work and other skills are reported by students to foster conditions whereby they can observe their own learning styles, change these styles to suit different tasks and engage more deeply with the content of their subject. These latter attributes are often cited as prerequisites for a deep approach to learning. This revitalized interest in key skills has succeeded in according group work a new status.

Despite moves towards mass participation and larger classes in higher education, the quality of the learning experience, the need to deliver key skills and the potential for innovation, have contributed to the retention and enhancement of the small group method. Small groups are used extensively, and in many different ways, eg, in problem-based learning approaches.

Planning

Successful small group teaching and learning does not happen by chance. Planning for effective small group teaching is as important as planning any other teaching activity. This point sometimes goes unrecognized because the actual activity of learning in small groups can at first glance appear unstructured. Some lecturers are put off by the seemingly informal, loose or open-ended nature of small group learning. Others fear this informality will be a recipe for chaos or that the group will develop into a therapy session. All types of teaching must be planned as part of a coherent package, with appropriate use of different methods within each component.

This appearance of informality is deceptive. Behind the facade of the informal group lies a backdrop in which all the learners are playing within a known set of rules which are spoken or unspoken. The approach might better be described as a kind of structured spontaneity. In other words, the creative flow of ideas is possible precisely because the lecturer or leader has a clear framework, deliberately planned to meet the objectives of the session. Within this framework, students feel safe to develop their ideas. Equally important, staff feel safe to try out and practise the skills of small group teaching.

Planning for small group teaching may take many forms. It will have much in common with features of planning for any learning occasion. Typically the teacher might consider the intended learning outcomes, selection of suitable type of small group teaching method and learner activity.

Beyond these general features the session plan will be dependent upon the requirements of specific disciplines, the culture of the institution, the overall context of the programme or module and the particular learning needs and prior knowledge of the students.

Whatever form the plan takes, it is critical that precise intentions for small group work are outlined. It is salutary to ask often whether what is being aimed at, and undertaken in small groups, is qualitatively different from that which is being carried out in other delivery modes. The gains for the students should justify the extra costs incurred. In short, the aims and content of the teaching session should dictate and justify the means.

Interrogating Practice

Using your own experience as a learner in small groups, identify strengths and weaknesses of different approaches used in your discipline.

Preparing Learners

In a study into peer tutoring in higher education staff indicated that they had recognized the need for student preparation on the ëknowledge of subjectí side but had not recognized, prior to their action research, the extent to which students would need training, and ongoing facilitation, to work in the new ways. These new ways refer to working within learner groups. This finding concurs with evidence from other quarters, where students offering advice to lecturers say that lecturers too often assume that they, the students, know how to work in groups. It is just as important for teaching staff to prepare students to work in groups as it is to prepare themselves. Interrogating Practice How do you assist learners to organize small group sessions where you are not present? How could you improve on your current practice? Preparing students to work in small groups can mean providing specific training for students on how groups work. Such training will develop an understanding that all groups go through a number of stages. Hence, when conflict arises in the group, for example, it can be understood and dealt with as a natural feature to be resolved, rather than perceived as a descent into chaos. Preparation can also mean affording structured opportunities at strategic points within the teaching programme to examine how the group is functioning, what problems exist and how resolution can be achieved. Some lecturers achieve this by providing guidelines (ground rules) at the beginning of a small group session or at the beginning of a series of seminars or workshops. Some lecturers go further, believing that students (either individually or as a group) can themselves effectively be involved in establishing and negotiating ground rules and intended outcomes. Such activities may constitute a learning contract. Such a learning contract is an important way of effecting a safe and supportive learning environment. Establishing the contract may involve tutors and students in jointly:

- Setting, agreeing and understanding objectives.
- Agreeing assessment procedures and criteria (if appropriate).
- Allocating tasks to all participants, tutors and students.

- Developing ground rules for behaviour within the group.

The staff/student contract provides a mechanism for continuing review. It is recommended that time be set aside every third or fourth meeting to evaluate the progress and process of the groupís working against the original contract.

Phases of Group Development

Social group theorists describe the initial phases in the life of a group using a variety of terms such as inclusion, forming and approach-avoid ambivalence. These works discuss the behaviour of individuals working in groups. What is also recognized is the conflicting tendency to avoid the situation of joining groups because of the demands, the frustration and even the pain it may bring about. This ëmoving towards, pulling awayí behaviour can easily create tension in the early stages of a group if it is not handled sensitively. Certain behaviours may be a natural part of the initial joining stages rather than a conscious act of defiance or withdrawal by a student. Understanding how students are likely to behave can assist the tutor to provide a framework that fosters confidence and allows trust to develop.

The ending of the group often brings to the surface many issues to do with termination. How intervention is handled at this stage will have a bearing on helping the members to move on. The tutor needs to be aware of appropriate ways of ending different types of group activity.

Interrogating Practice

Consider small group teaching sessions you have facilitated. Think about the different types of individual and group behaviour you have witnesses. What were the possible causes?

Significance of the Setting

Few tutors in higher education work in an ideal setting with tailor-designed group workrooms. A great deal can be done, however, in setting up the room to encourage participation and interaction. The research into the influence of environmental factors on interaction has been fairly extensive and shows that physical arrangements have a powerful effect. For example, Korda documents the effect on encounters when one person is seated and the other is not. It is well known that communication increases if the differences in social level or status are small. Therefore, part of the tutorís task is to play down the differences in roles and, in particular, play down his or her own authority. This will facilitate the free flow of discussion. It is not a straightforward matter since the tutor must relinquish authority while all the time remaining in control. This knowledge about the need to minimize social status differences has an impact on where the tutor actually sits within the group. In fact, it is possible to arrange a room so that certain desired effects are achieved. Three situations serve as examples of this point:

- Nervous students can be encouraged to participate more readily if their place in the group is opposite (i.e., in direct eye-contact) to either a sympathetic tutor or an encouraging, more voluble student peer.
- A dominating, vociferous student can be quiet ended by being seated immediately next to the tutor.
- The level of student participation and of student-student interaction can be affected by the choice of room itself. Is the tutorís own room with all his or her paraphernalia of authority likely to be more or less conducive to student participation? What is an unadorned, stark seminar room with a rectangular table and a special high-backed lectureris chair at one end likely to dictate for the processes of the group?

Interrogating Practice

Visualize yourself in a room where you teach small groups. Where should you sit to maximize your interaction with the group? Where might a student sit to avoid interaction with the tutor or with other students? Where might a student sit if he or she wishes to persuade others of a point of view?

Types of Small Group Teaching

A specific method selected for small group teaching will derive from the objectives set. There are many different methods of small group teaching; some methods are more suited to certain disciplines than others. However, few methods are peculiar to one subject alone. A large number of methods can be adapted for use in any subject. It is important to remain flexible and open to try out a variety of methods drawn from a wide repertoire. It may be necessary to overcome a tendency to find one method that works well and use this method frequently. The effect on learners of over-exposure to one method of teaching is worth considering. Below is a brief description of various ways of working with small groups. It is not intended to be comprehensive, nor are all types mutually exclusive. Some methods are described in terms of a special setting that encourages the application of principles or techniques; for example, brainstorming is a structured setting for the use of lateral thinking. Other methods are described in terms of their size or purpose:

- *Brainstorm session*-generation of ideas from the group to foster lateral thinking. There is no criticism of ideas until they are logged.
- *Buzz group*-two or three people are asked to discuss an issue for a few minutes. Comments are usually then shared with a larger group.
- *Cross-over groups*-used for brief discussions then transfers between groups.

- *Fishbowl*-small groups are formed within a large, observation group, followed by discussion and reversal.
- *Free discussion*-topic and direction comes from the group; the tutor or leader observes.
- *Open-ended enquiries*-students determine the structure as well as reporting back on outcomes.
- *Peer tutoring*-students learn from one another and teach one another.
- *Problem-based tutorial group*-involves small groups using problem-based learning.
- *Role-play*-use of allocated or self-created roles. It is important to facilitate students to enter and come out of role.
- *Self-help group*-run by and for students; the tutor may be a resource.
- *Seminar*-group discussion of a paper presented by a student (note that this term is often used in different ways).
- *Simulation/game*-structured experience in real/imaginary roles. Guidelines on the process are important and feedback is critical.
- *Snowballing*-pairs become small groups then become larger groups.
- *Step-by-step discussion*-a planned sequence of issues/questions led by student or tutor.
- *Structured enquiries*-the tutor provides lightly structured experiments and guidance.
- *Syndicate*-involving mini-project work, followed by reporting to the full class.
- *Tutorial*-a meeting with a very small group, often based on feedback to an essay or assignment (note that this term is often used in different ways).
- *Tutorless group*-the group appoints a leader and may report back; may focus on discussion or completion of some other type of set task.

There are several approaches not mentioned above that can be used in small or large groups. The main determining factor is the amount of interaction that is desirable. Apart from that it is necessary to ensure that in a larger group all members can see, hear, and so on.

Skills for Effective Small Group Teaching

Among important skills for teachers, those of listening, asking and answering questions and responding are paramount in small group settings.

Questioning

The skills of asking and answering questions are not as simple as they might appear at face value. Many general teaching and social skills communication texts deal with the skill of questioning, for example Brown and Atkins. Good questioning techniques require continuing preparation, practice and reflection by students and teachers alike. Preparation of a repertoire of questions in advance will allow the teacher to work effectively and flexibly in the small group.

Similarly, student-to-student interactions in groups is enhanced if students prepare questions at the outset or end of a class. The confidence of students is often boosted through preparation of content in the form of key and incisive questions on a topic.

The type of question asked is also linked to promoting or inhibiting learning. Questions may be categorized in different ways such as:

Open	Closed
Broad	Narrow
Clear	Confused
Simple	Complex
Reflective	Recall
Probing	Superficial
Divergent	Convergent

Interrogating Practice

Broadly speaking, which categories do your questions fit into? Make a list of probing questions relevant to an important concept in your subject.

How you ask questions is also important in fostering student responses. Body language displaying an indifferent, aggressive, closed or anxious manner will be less effective. An open, warm challenging or sensitive manner may gain more responses of a thoughtful nature.

When asked a question by a student what are some of the things you can do other than directly answering the question?

The above activity concentrates on your reactions to student questions. Some of these reactions may result in students being able to answer their own questions. However, there will be times when you will directly answer the question. Directly answering questions during a group meeting takes less time than attempting to encourage the student or group to come up with the answers. If you choose to answer directly make your answer brief and to the point. After responding you may wish to check that you have really answered the question by saying some-thing like: ëDoes that answer your question?í The timing of asking questions, the use of pause and silence are also important in developing the skills of answering and asking questions. Taking these matters into consideration may in part address the common problem teachers in higher education report-that students do not contributc during small group sessions.

Listening

The mental process of listening is an active one that calls into play a number of thinking functions including analysis, comprehension, synthesis and evaluation. Genuine listening also has an emotional dimension since it requires an ability to share, and quite possibly understand, another personís feelings, and understand his or her situation. Intellectual and emotional meanings are communicated by the listener and speaker in both verbal and non-verbal forms. So how you listen will be observable through gestures and body language. Your listening skills may be developed by thinking about all the levels of a studentís comment, in this way:

- What is said: the content;
- How it is said: tone and feelings;
- When it is said: time and priority;
- Where it is said: place and environment.

Listening attentively to individual students in the group and to the groupís mood will heighten your ability to respond. This may require a new approach, one that demands practising silence, but if you persevere you will find this an attainable skill, through which remarkable insights can be gained.

Interrogating Practice

Consider how much time you spend listening to students and encouraging students to listen to one another. Check out your perceptions of your real talk time/listening time by asking students for feedback.

Responding

Listening in silence by paying undivided attention to the speaker is an active process, engaging and heightening awareness and observation. The other aspect of positive listening is of course to intervene in a variety of ways for a variety of purposes. The more intense our listening is, the more likely it is that we will know how to respond, when to respond and in what ways.

There are many ways of responding and many reasons for responding in a certain way Appropriate responses are usually made when the tutor has considered not only the cognitive aims of the session but also the interpersonal needs of the group and the individual learnerís level of confidence and knowledge. Different responses will have different consequences for the individual student and for the behaviour of the group as a whole. Therefore, an appropriate response can only be deemed appropriate in the context of the particular small group teaching session.

Interrogating Practice

Along with a small group of colleagues, determine what skills you might usefully develop to increase effectiveness as a facilitator of groups.

8

Managing Quality and Standards in Chemistry Teaching

Introduction

It is important to come to some agreement about terminology and definitions of quality and standards as these concepts underpin the thinking behind the design, delivery, assessment and review of educational provision. The development of shared language includes the adoption of a technical language drawn largely from industry that now determines how higher education institutions discuss and understand ëqualityí. Definitions and usage of the terms ëstandardsí and ëqualityí vary and may depend on the aims and purposes of the educational provision or country and historical context. In the UK at present, ëstandardsí usually refers to expected or actual student attainment in terms of grading of performance. Quality is used in an even broader manner and with much variability in meaning, and may refer to a number of things, including individual student performance, the outputs of an educational programme, the student learning experience, the teaching provided, etc. The concept of quality can be sub-divided into several categories, as Harvey, Burrows and Green demonstrated, including:

- Quality as excellence-the traditional (often implicit) academic view which aims to demonstrate high academic standards.
- Quality as ëzero errorsí-most relevant in mass industry where detailed product specifications can be established and standardized measurements of uniform products can show conformity to them, but in higher education might be applied, eg, to learning materials.
- Quality as ëfitness for purposesí-focuses on ëcustomersí (or stakeholders) ëneedsí (eg, of students, employers, the academic community, government, or society), and/or as defined by the stated aims and learning outcomes of a programme of study. In the last decade, in the UK, this has been the dominant usage of the word ëqualityí.
- Quality as enhancement-emphasizes continuous improvement.
- Quality as transformation-applies either to studentsí behaviour and goals changing as a result of their studies or to socio-political transformation achieved through higher education.
- Quality as threshold-refers to meeting a minimum standard, as in subject benchmarking. Minimum standards are defined in most European higher education systems to enable a minimum, objective comparability of units or programmes. It is expected that minimum standards will be surpassed.

Interrogating Practice

Looking at the different definitions of ëqualityí, which of these best describe how teaching quality is talked about in your department?

The term quality assurance refers to the policies, processes and actions through which quality is maintained and developed. Evaluation is a key part of quality assurance. Accountability and enhancement are important motives for quality assurance. Accountability in this context refers to assuring students, society and government that quality is well managed. Quality enhancement refers to the improvement of quality e.g., through dissemination of good practice or use of a continuous improvement cycle. The purpose of internally driven quality assurance is usually to effect an improvement in the functioning of a department or programme, whereas externally driven review is generally more about accountability. Quality assurance is not new in higher education, for example external examiners as part of assessment processes, and the peer review system for research publications, are quality assurance processes that have been present for many years.

Accreditation is recognition that provision meets certain standards, and may in some instances confer a licence to operate. The status may have consequences for the institution itself and/or its students (eg, eligibility for grants) and/or its graduates (eg, making them qualified for certain employment).

A set of performance indicators (PIs) generally form part of a quality assurance system. PIs are a numerical measure of outputs of a system or institution in terms of the unitís goals (e.g., increasing employability of graduates, minimizing drop-out) or the educational processes (e.g., maximizing student satisfaction, minimizing cancelled lectures). Other indicators, not directly linked to performance, might include staff-student ratios and availability of learning resources for students. In developing a set of indicators, the aim is to find a balance between measurability (reliability), which is often the prime consideration in developing indicators, and relevance (validity). It is difficult to decide how to weight or combine indicators and indicators should be viewed as signals that show where strengths and weaknesses may be found, not as quality judgements in themselves.

The Bologna Declaration emphasizes the importance of a common framework for European higher education qualifications. In the UK a number of initiatives are being taken to help to ensure comparability between programmes in terms of standards, levels and credits.

Arrangements for quality assurance vary between countries, but many have created national agencies.

The National Context

Higher education in the UK is undergoing much rapid change. The massification of the system, widening participation, and the falling unit of resource have been among issues contributing to concern about maintaining and enhancing educational quality. This has contributed since the 1980s to government placing heavier emphasis on higher education being accountable for the public money it spends, on demonstrating quality, and on specification of outcomes. The evolution of the means by which government has required higher education to demonstrate and be assessed for quality in relation to education have been succinctly described by Middlehurst, in the first edition of this handbook. It is convenient for the purposes of this chapter to take up that story in 1997.

The National Committee of Inquiry into Higher Education (NCIHE) reviewed UK higher education. The NCIHE published its findings and recommendations in the Dearing Report. The report made wide-ranging recommendations including the framework for a new ëquality agendaí, the establishment of a professional body for teachers in higher education and the formalizing of subject discipline networks. These resulted in the establishment of the Institute for Learning and Teaching in Higher Education (ILT) and the Learning and Teaching Support Network (LTSN) in 1999.

The ILT, a professional membership body, has responsibility for accrediting individuals and programmes in teaching and learning in higher education against criteria that emphasize reflective practice and an understanding of the philosophy and learning methods appropriate to the sector. The subject centres of the LTSN are not involved in assuring the quality of programmes, but in quality enhancement through support of lecturers in their teaching role-by facilitating the sharing and dissemination of up-to-date information through conferences, Web sites and journals. Membership of the ILT and involvement in the work of LTSNs are quality indicators relating to teaching staff.

The QAA was formed in 1997. The QAA was contracted by the Funding Councils to carry out audits and assessments of the quality of education in publicly funded institutions on their behalf. Audit was concerned with verifying that academic procedures were as declared. Teaching assessment was concerned with provision at subject level and brought virtually all academics in England into contact with QAA processes. Over time the precise details of teaching assessment changed. Although slightly different methods were used in Scotland and Wales, the concept of using external review teams who were experts in their subject discipline was central to all teaching assessment processes. The teams of reviewers were selected from subject disciplines and led by a chair who was not a subject expert but whose role was to ensure adherence to the process and method.

Training Subject Reviewers

Between 1994 and 2002, some 4,500 academics, clinicians and professional practitioners have been trained to undertake subject level quality reviews across UK higher education. A mixed team of QAA officers, experienced review coordinators and senior staff from the Higher Education Staff Development Agency, delivers training, typically of two-three daysí duration. Although each funding council has its own processes and emphases, the approach described below provides a general sense of the training and the significance attached to it. Training is offered to potential reviewers after a rigorous selection process and it is a condition of appointment that all individuals undertake the training. This not only ensures effective induction to the role and initial consistency in briefing, but also provides an opportunity for prospective reviewers to be observed in simulated situations prior to work in the sector. The overall aim of training has been to produce individuals who understand and are committed to the review method and who are competent to undertake the range of duties required of them. Minimally, the reviewing role entails:

- a secure grasp of the processes and values underpinning the review method;
- familiarity with reference documentation, eg, the QAA Code of Practice, appropriate subject benchmarks;
- well-founded skills of analysis, information management and a capacity to make evidence-based judgements;
- effective communication and interpersonal skills to manage meetings with colleagues, peers, students and, possibly, employers;
- drafting and report writing skills necessary to contribute to the production of a report in the style and to the specification required by the QAA;
- a capacity to work accurately under pressure and to maintain a professional manner.

This particular amalgam of knowledge, understandings, skills and attitudes cannot be developed by a didactic approach; thus training is shaped by a strong philosophical commitment to use of a wide range of learning formats. The key vehicle for learning is an extensive simulation exercise. Reviewers are required to complete an initial personal analysis of preparatory materials before training commences. This preparation feeds into a simulated team meeting in which reviewers identify significant issues for further enquiry. Subsequently, reviewers are provided with opportunities to conduct meetings with ëstaffï and ëstudentsí, to analyse samples of studentsí work, to revise their agenda in the light of cumulative evidence, to begin drafting a report and to engage with making judgements. These practical activities, undertaken on an individual and small group basis, are interspersed with brief informational inputs to highlight important issues, key processes, appropriate protocols and core values. Every training event is evaluated and feedback is sought from participants on its perceived relevance and effectiveness in equipping them with the skills they need. Feedback has been consistently positive with 96 per cent of participants rating the training in the highest category Participants indicate that reviewer training achieves its immediate objectives, but also provides an opportunity to think more generally about issues of curriculum design, approaches to assessment, the determination of standards of achievement, student support, mechanisms for quality improvement and the effective deployment of learning resources. As such, reviewer training produces individuals who are equipped to act as a resource with their immediate colleagues for local benefit, as well as contributing formally to a sector-wide system. In this sense, reviewer training is a powerful form of updating for experienced staff in mid to late career. Subject review examined six aspects of provision relating to learning and teaching:

- curriculum design and organization;
- teaching, learning and assessment;
- student progression and achievement;
- student support and guidance;
- learning resources;
- quality management and enhancement.

Visits normally took place over four days and in order to triangulate evidence (i.e., obtain evidence from a range of sources) carried out a number of activities in reaching a judgement:

- documentary review, including a self-assessment document by the subject team and documents relating to the six aspects in a base room;
- formal meetings with staff and students covering the six aspects;
- meetings with senior managers and others;
- direct observation of teaching and learning events;
- visits to facilities and learning resources such as libraries, computer laboratories and other teaching rooms.

In England a numerical score for each aspect of provision was awarded. Written reports were produced for each visit, summarizing the main strengths and areas for improvement.

Contemporary Quality Agenda

There was extensive debate about a replacement for subject review, with much discussion of reduction in external scrutiny and bureaucracy and an increase in institutional autonomy and quality as enhancement (rather than as inspection). New arrangements for 2002-03 onwards look likely to place greater emphasis on compliance with externally determined and audited standards and norms, but to have a lighter ëinspectoriali touch. The new agenda can be described as a ëjigsawí comprising interdependent and interlocking processes that emphasize increasing transparency, accountability and specification.

The main elements of the quality framework will be a combination of institutional audit (at the level of the whole organization) and academic review (at the level of the subject discipline). Audit will have a ëlighter touchí and follow up areas of concern, consistent with the principle of intervention in inverse proportion to success. There will be an increased emphasis on public access to: ëeasily understood, reliable and meaningful public information about the extent to which institutions are individually offering programmes of study, awards and qualifications that meet general national expectations in respect of academic standards and qualityí.

This will place considerable demands on lecturers and other staff. Examples of information likely to have to be provided include details of internal assurance processes, student evaluations, student satisfaction surveys, employersí evaluations and input to programme, examinersí reports (internal and external), intake and graduate data and more detailed information concerning programme content and assessment. There is also likely to be scrutiny of provision and take-up of staff development and training, particularly in the area of teaching and learning, including membership of a professional body such as the ILT, as these may be seen as quality indicators at institutional and departmental level. QAA teams will consider how institutions have put into practice the new national requirements including:

- The publication of and adherence to a Learning and Teaching Strategy and use of the associated Teaching Quality Enhancement Funds.
- The use of external reference points including the Code of Practice for the assurance of academic quality and standards in higher education, the Framework for Higher Education Qualifications in England, Wales and Northern Ireland and subject benchmark statements.
- The development, use and publication of programme specifications and progress files.

Framework for Higher Education Qualifications (FHEQ)

The FHEQ was finalized in 2001 and aims to inform employers, students and other stakeholders about the levels that holders of a qualification have achieved and what skills they bring to a job. The framework simplifies the range of awards and describes five levels of achievement: three at Bacheloris degree level which correspond to three years of study but incorporate the shorter ëfoundationí degrees, one at Masters and one at Doctoral level. Generic statements indicate the levels of achievement expected within these awards, whatever the subject.

The FHEQ aims to assure the public that qualifications from different institutions and for different subjects represent similar levels of achievement. The levels are reference points to determine whether the intended learning outcomes for a programme are appropriate to the level of the qualification awarded. The external examiner system will become increasingly important as a means of comparison between programmes at different institutions. Lecturers and institutions will need to ensure their programmes match the appropriate level.

Programme Specifications

In 1999 the QAA stated: ëprogramme specifications are an essential part of the strategy for helping higher education to make the outcomes of learning more explicit and permit the programmes and awards to be related to the Qualifications Frameworkí.

In a programme specification, teaching teams are expected to set out:

- The intended learning outcomes of a programme (specific, measurable intentions expressed in terms of what learners will be able to do (*a*) as knowledge and understanding and (*b*) as skills and other attributes).

- The teaching and learning methods that enable learners to do this.
- The assessment methods used to demonstrate the achievement of learning outcomes.
- The relationship of the programme and its study elements to the FHEQ.

Programme specifications affect the work of individual lecturers and course teams directly, as they must produce and amend them (often using an institution-wide format), and then expect judgements to be made against them by the university (through its quality assurance committees and boards), students, employers and external reviewers. Their production requires the essential elements of a programme to be synthesized into a short space, no matter what its complexity

Subject Benchmarking

Subject benchmarks describe general expectations about the standards, attributes and capabilities relating to the award of qualifications at a given level in a particular subject area. They were produced by groups of senior academics in each subject, in consultation with the sector. They are statements about ëthreshold qualityí or ëminimum standardsí. For example, in medicine: ëthe benchmarks for medical degrees have been defined in terms of the intellectual attributes, the knowledge and understanding, the clinical, interpersonal and practical skills, and the professional competencies which will allow the graduates to function effectively as pre-registration house officers and develop as professionalsí.

Subject benchmark statements are used in conjunction with the FHEQ. For any given programme there should be compatibility between the intended learning outcomes and the relevant programme specification. Lecturers need to be aware of the benchmark statements for their own subjects, particularly if they are involved in curriculum design or the production of programme specifications. Statements can be used as a checklist when designing new programmes or when reviewing the content of existing curricula. The benchmark statements will be used by external bodies as reference points for checking purposes.

Interrogating Practice

How do/might the programme specification(s) and subject benchmark statements relevant to your teaching help you day-to-day, e.g., in planning teaching sessions or designing assessments? What advantages and disadvantages can you see to an ëoutcomes based approachí?

Progress files (PFs)

The PF has two elements. From 2002-03 the transcript or academic record element of the PF will be produced by institutions. It records student achievement according to a common format and contains details of the courses/modules taken by a student (including the results of assessment). The second part of the PF is owned and produced by the student and is termed personal development planning (PDP). PDP will facilitate students to monitor, build and reflect on their development. PDP should be fully implemented by 2005-06 and institutions must provide the opportunity for students to undertake PDP Staff will need to ensure that adequate, appropriate and timely assessment information is provided for the transcript. The precise degree of involvement and encouragement that academic or support staff may make to PDP is not yet clear, and may vary between institutions and disciplines. For example, it may be used as a means of structuring tutorials or meetings with individual students, and different types of PDP may be developed, ranging from a highly reflective ëjournalí or diary to a more prosaic, descriptive record of development and skill acquisition. Issues of confidentiality and responsibility are likely to arise. In many institutions PDP will be electronic, but teachers will need to be aware of the format and process by which it is managed at their own institution.

Interrogating Practice

Has PDP been introduced into your institution? If so, how useful do students find it as a tool for developing a reflective approach to study and development? How do/might you as a teacher help students to use PDP for personal and professional development?

The external examiner system

The QAA plans to use external examining as a key element of ensuring quality and standards. Work will be carried out to ensure that the external examiner system is operating so as to ensure public confidence in academic quality and standards. Summaries of external examiner reports will be published as part of the audit process.

Public information: student satisfaction surveys

A key plank of the new quality arrangements is the requirement for institutions to make a range of information (such as programme specifications) widely available to various types of ëcustomerí of higher education. Student ratings are one such area. At time of publication exact requirements in this area are still changing, but some form of student satisfaction data, broader than feedback on specific modules, is likely to be required.

Lecturers (and administrators) need to be aware that there may be national and institutional requirements on them to participate in the collection of data from students, to respond to the comments received, and to ensure that information is made available for public consumption.

The Student Satisfaction Approach at the University of Central England (UCE), Birmingham

The Satisfaction Approach has been developed at the Centre for Research into Quality over the last 15 years. The approach was designed to be an effective tool with which to obtain, analyse and report studentsí views of their total university experience in order to effect change and improvement. Student Satisfaction has evolved into a major quality and planning tool at UCE as part of a process of continuous quality improvement. It is a template for ëqualityí information requirements in this area.

The Student Satisfaction Approach is a market leader and has been emulated and adapted by a number of higher and further education institutions both in the UK and overseas (including New Zealand, Sweden, Australia, South Africa, Hong Kong and Poland).

The methodology continues to evolve and allows the surveys to be flexible to address the pressing concerns of students. The methodology can be easily adapted to different situations. It has been used to explore the views of a variety of stakeholders: staff, postgraduate research students, employers, placement supervisors and even football supporters. The Student Satisfaction approach is unique in combining the following four elements:

- Student-determined questions: the Student Satisfaction research focuses on the total learning experience as defined by students (via focus groups or in-depth interviews).
- Satisfaction *and* importance ratings: the research examines student satisfaction with aspects of provision and then identifies which of those areas are important for students.
- Management information for action: those areas which are important to students but where students are dissatisfied are priority areas for management intervention.
- A clear feedback and action cycle.

Management information

The items in the survey that are unsatisfactory but important for students become target items for action.

Satisfaction data is also mapped longitudinally, which allows for benchmarking of improvement in student satisfaction year by year.

The survey results are reported to the Vice-Chancellor and, through him, to the Board of Governors and Senate. They are published in an annual report from the Centre. A central feature of the report is the composite rating tables and trend graphs, which clearly identify areas for action and trends, without lots of impenetrable statistics.

Action and feedback

At the centre of the process is the action and feedback cycle. The intention is that there is a process that identifies responsibility for action and subsequent follow-up to ensure action takes place.

The internal consultation process at UCE reviews action from previous years and prioritizes action based on student views, which is linked to budget allocation letters. The Vice-Chancellor interviews all the deans and heads of services about the outcomes of the report, who are required to indicate what action they are intending to take and what has happened as a result of the previous yearís agenda. The replies are made available to Senate for discussion and a summary of action taken is communicated back to students.

Transitional arrangements

It is envisaged that in the transitional period from 2002-04 the QAA will engage with institutions to carry out institutional audits and to participate in discipline-based review or activity, which for most institutions will take the form of new, development-focused engagements intended to test internal procedures for assuring quality and standards. A limited number of academic reviews will also be carried out during the transition period.

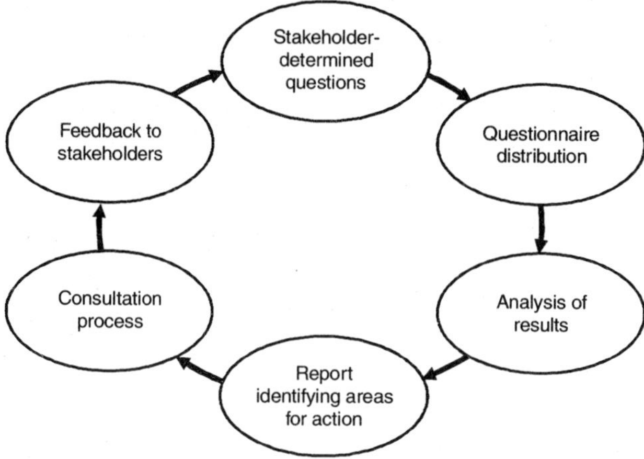

Figure 8.1. Satisfaction cycle

Institutional audit

By the middle of the first decade of the 21st century national quality arrangements are likely to mean that there will normally be one institutional audit visit by an external review team on a five- or six-yearly cycle, focusing on the whole institution. The expectation is that the institution will be expected to produce a self-evaluation document (SED) approximately 13 weeks before the visit. Audits will consider several examples of the institutionís quality assurance processes at work, at the level of the programme (ëdiscipline audit trailsí-approximately 10 per cent of programmes in terms of full-time equivalent student numbers-or across the whole organization -íthematic enquiriesí). The audit team in consultation with the institution will select enquiries and trails. The capacity to ëdrill downí through academic review at subject level in cases where the reviewers have concerns will remain, despite the main emphasis being at institutional rather than subject level. Each audit is likely to comprise two visits, a short briefing visit, and five weeks later, the audit visit itself, normally five days. One of the main tasks of the audit team will be to consider the internal processes and outcomes of periodic quality assurance reviews of programmes/discipline areas. The audit team will seek to establish whether procedures are robust enough to ensure and enhance educational quality across all the provision that the institution manages. The audit will consider:

- the accuracy, completeness and reliability of published information about programmes and the standards of awards;
- the academic standards expected of and achieved by students;
- the experience of students as ìearners;
- the quality assurance of staff, including appointment criteria and the ways in which teaching effectiveness is appraised, improved and rewarded.

Audit teams will meet with staff and students, undertake documentary analysis (which will include samples of assessed student work and external examiner reports) in the course of discipline audit trails, and explore issues and procedures relating to internal quality assurance. Shortly after the visit, the audit team will summarize the main findings and recommendations, and produce a draft report. The final public report will state the level of confidence the audit team has in the provision. If the report contains positive statements of confidence and no recommendations for action then the audit will be formally ësigned off on publication and there will be limited follow up with the QAA. If statements of confidence are qualified or recommendations suggest important weaknesses that should be urgently addressed, the report will be published but there will be a programme of follow-up action, including a revisit after one year to consider the institutionís action plan and adherence to it. It is likely that in time, the audit process will have aí lighter touchí for institutions that demonstrate they have sound quality assurance and enhancement mechanisms.

Interrogating Practice

How are the processes of institutional audit and academic review impacting on your work?

Enhancing and Managing Quality

It is often hard for individual academics to make connections between their fundamental concern to do a good job for their own and their studentsí satisfaction, and the mechanisms and requirements associated with the ëquality banneri. But educational quality can (and should) be seen as everyoneís responsibility.

At institutional level, arrangements must be set in place for the formal management of quality and standards in accordance with the national agenda described above. External reviews by the QAA and PSBs (e.g., in medicine or engineering) are often used by institutions as a framework for internal quality management and can provide a focus and milestone towards which many institutions work.

The institution will have a formal committee structure, part of whose function is to manage and monitor quality, including external examining. This is usually supported by an administrative function (often in Registry) to collect and collate data relating to academic quality, e.g., student feedback questionnaires, annual course reviews, admissions or examination statistics. Structures and processes vary between institutions, but they should enable issues concerning educational quality to be identified in a timely and appropriate way and be dealt with. One of the senior management team (e.g., a pro vice-chancellor) normally has an identified remit for ensuring educational quality and maintaining academic standards. Clear mechanisms for the approval of new programmes and a regular system of programme reviews should be in place. One of the fundamental elements of quality assurance is to enable feedback (from students, staff, employers and external reviewers) to be considered and issues addressed.

Additional formal mechanisms usually operate at faculty and departmental level in order to enable the consideration of more detailed issues and to address concerns more speedily Committees (such as teaching and learning committees) include representatives from programmes. They act to promulgate, interpret and implement organizational strategy, policies and procedures; to develop and implement procedures for managing the monitoring and review of faculty/departmental programmes and procedures; and to respond to demands from review, accreditation or inspection bodies. Staff-student liaison committees are another example of committees operating at this (or programme) level.

It is at programme level where the individual teacher will be mainly involved in ensuring the quality of provision. All those who teach need to be committed to and understand the purposes and context of the programmes on offer, and be aware of the elements that may comprise a ëqualityí learning experience for students. They will also need to be familiar with and understand the use of programme specifications, levels, benchmarking, etc. Those teaching on a programme will be required to have formal monitoring and review systems to consider all activity relating to learning and the learning environment, including administrative procedures (such as ensuring that assessment results are collected and analysed or that course materials are distributed in a timely fashion). Delivering a good ëstudent learning experienceí requires a high level of competence and understanding: formal education about teaching and learning in higher education.

Interrogating Practice

Do you know how the systems of feedback and quality management (e.g., committee structures, external examining, and feedback loops) work in your department and institution?

Internal quality assurance procedures and development activities to enhance educational quality are likely to include the evaluation of individual staff members through systems such as student feedback questionnaires, peer review systems, mentoring for new staff or regular appraisals.

Conclusion

Assuring and enhancing educational quality and academic standards can be seen as complex and multifaceted activities, but at the centre of these are the individual learner and lecturer. Higher education in the UK is largely funded by public money and students as fee payers have a set of often ill-defined expectations relating to their programme of learning. The new quality agenda firmly sets out to make higher education more transparent and accountable and to define the outcomes of learning programmes more specifically. Awareness of the concepts, terminology and expectations of national agencies concerned with quality, coupled with increasing competence and understanding of teaching and learning processes can help the individual teacher and course team member to contribute effectively towards the development and enhancement of a quality culture in higher education.

❑❑❑

9

Periodic System in Chemistry

Introduction

The properties of the elements are similar and the atomic weight of the middle element is higher than that of the first member of the group by as much as it is lower than that of the last. At least such a rule seemed to exist; in some cases a more precise revision of the atomic weights might, he hoped, confirm it.

The search for such rules was greatly stimulated by William Proutís hypothesis that all atoms were built of primordial atoms which he tried to identify with the hydrogen atom. Berzelius ridiculed ìthe fever of the multiples,î but it received strong support from the new development in organic chemistry. Organic radicals had been compared with elements as a kind of justification for that hypothetical concept. Now the process was reversed. Max Pettenkofer, in Munich, compared metals with organic radicals in order to find ìthe regular distances of the so-called simple radicalsî (1850). J.B. Dumas applied the theory of organic types to elements. He saw the ìtype of fluorineî in the other halogens, and the ìtype of azoteî in phosphorus, arsenic, and antimony. Such groups of elements form a progression, like homologous organic compounds. When a = initial number or type, d = the difference in atomic weights, and n = the consecutive number of an element, the progression is $a + nd$, and nd defines the place of the member.

These attempts suffered from the unsettled state between atomic and equivalent weights. As long as Cl was given by the atomic weight 35.5, while oxygen was considered as having the atomic weight 8, or magnesium 12 and chromium 26, no reasonable rules for progressions could be formed. The agreement reached through Cannizzaroís return to Avogadroís and Dulongís theory cleared the way for further efforts. Dumas and Stas, who worked on precise methods for determining atomic weights, arrived at a confirmation of Doebereineris hypothesis of the constant increments in triads.

BÈguyer de Chancourtois devised an arrangement of all elements along a ìtelluric helix,î a spiral cut at an angle of 45 on a cylinder mantle. John A.R. Newlands, a practical sugar chemist published a table in which sixty-two elements were listed in the order of atomic weights. They were divided into eight vertical columns and seven horizontal families. The number eight seemed to him of deep importance; the relation of the number of analogous elements is that of one or more octaves in music. The first element in the row is similar to the eighth. The relationship to musical octaves, which might have been full of hidden meaning to men of earlier centuries, as it obviously was to Newlands, seemed to discredit his efforts in the eyes of his contemporaries who were not ready either to accept de Chancourtoisí assertion that ìthe properties of the substances are the properties of the numbersî.

Just at this time a small book by Julius Lothar Meyer 1830-1895, T¸bingen) was published in Breslau on *The Modern Theories of Chemistry*, with a table of twenty-eight elements. They were arranged in six horizontal rows in the order of the atomic weights, and in six vertical columns according to their valency.

At that time it was not possible to include all the known elements because the atomic weights for some of them were doubtful or erroneous. Tallium was only tentatively included at a place in the column where the alkali metals were listed. It was a continuation of Doebereineris attempt to discover the significance of the differences between the atomic weights in the vertical columns.

In 1868 Dmitri Ivanovich Mendeleyev undertook to write a handbook of chemistry and needed a system of the simple bodies for its organization. In this predicament, which recalls that of Berzelius about sixty years before, Mendeleyev decided to base his system on an absolutely objective principle, the atomic weights. At night, in his sleep, he saw the periodicity with which similar elements recur. In March, 1869, he presented his first periodic table to the Russian Chemical Society. It contained question marks and empty spaces for undiscovered elements. ìThe boldness of thoughtî which he ascribed to himself proved successful. ìThe elements, arranged according to the order of their atomic weights, represent a clearly recognizable periodicity of the properties. The magnitude of the atomic weight determines the character of the elements. We must expect the discovery of many unknown simple substances, e.g., analogues of aluminum and silicium with the atomic weight 65-75. Some analogies of the elements are discovered by their atomic weights.î This is the *Natural System of the Elements*. He used it to predict the properties of undiscovered elements and his predictions were confirmed when scandium, gallium and germanium were actually discovered. This method of predicting properties from the place in the system was of great help in later work on rare gases and radioactively produced elements. Physical properties, like specific heat, light refraction, melting point, ductility, and metallic character, and conductivity for heat and electricity were found by Meyer and Mendeleyev to be functions of the atomic weights. ìThe numerical value of the atomic weights is the variable by which the material nature and the related properties are determined. Mendeleyev discarded all ìdeeperî speculation about the reasons for periodicity; Meyer felt that Proutís hypothesis might hold the key for an explanation. He found some of Mendeleyevís arrangements of the elements unwarranted and disturbing, and he warned against ìunnecessary hypotheses.î Mendeleyev quickly accepted the criticism of his first table, and so corrected the positions of several elements in his large table of 1870.

Lothar Meyer's Table (1864)

4-Valent	3-Valent	2-Valent	1-Valent	1-Valent	2-Valent
-	-	-	-	Li 7.01	(Be) (9.3)
Diff.=				15.98	(14.6)
C 11.97	N 14.01	O 15.96	Fl 19.1	Na 22.99	Mg 23.94
Diff.=16	16.95	16.02	16.3	16.05	15.96
Si 28	P 30.96	S 31.98	Cl 35.37	K 39.04	Ca 39.90
	43.9	46	44.38	46.2	17.3
-	As 74.9	Se 78	Br 79.75	Rb 85.2	Sr 87.2
Diff.=45	47	50	46.78	47.5	49.6
Sn 117.8	Sb 122	Te 128	J 126.53	Cs 132.7	Ba1 36.8
Diff.=88.6	85.5				
Pb 206.4	Bi 207.5	-	-	Tl 204?	-

Above all the differences in the details and in the distinction between fact and hypothesis, it was now established that ìthe properties of the elements are closely related to the atomic weight; they are functions, and periodic functions at that, of the magnitude of the atomic weight.î

Mendeleyev was satisfied with the beauty of a relationship which embraced the actually known elements and formed the systematic rule to which any possible element was subject. If Proutís hypothesis could be verified, which would mean that all elements are built of hydrogen atoms, it would indicate a homology between the elements but not a periodicity. The determination of atomic weights to which Stas devoted his efforts seemed to leave the hypothesis at least debatable for a long time. Finally, however, Stas came to the conclusion that exceptions to the rule were too frequent and too unquestionable to keep it up any longer, and he had to give up his Conviction which he had set out to prove.

The spectra of some elements at high temperatures were interpreted as indicating a decomposition into other elements, but this was refuted. V. von Richter summed these experiences up in the following words: ìWhile thus no actual proof of the possibility of decomposition of elements is available, and while a synthesis of elements is still further away than their real dissection, this does not at all impose a limit to speculation. It appears as the task of theoretical chemistry in this direction first to find the real law of atomic numbers, then to develop a hypothesis which is satisfactory for explaining the properties of the elements on the assumption of one, or perhaps several, primordial substances in a manner similar to that used for the carbon compounds. At any rate, it is even now established that the qualities of the elements can be related to quantities ólike colors to vibrationsóand that this goal of all scientific explanation of nature is also attainable with regard to the chemical elements.î

❑❑❑

10

Organic Chemistry

Introduction

All the organic compounds could be defined by the number and the arrangement of the atoms of carbon and a few other elements, mainly hydrogen, oxygen, and nitrogen, in the molecule of the substances. Since about 1870 it had become necessary to include the arrangement of the atoms in three-dimensional space as one of the variables and the concept of valence had to be enlarged by finer differentiations. Fundamentally, however, the principles of organic chemistry remained unchanged. The number of pure organic substances separated from natural materials and produced by artificial synthesis grew into many hundreds of thousands. The more chemical reactions that were found for the identification and production of compounds, the easier it became to determine the chemical structure of highly complex substances and to reach a final proof for the structure by synthesis in well-defined steps.

The meticulous care in developing methods for analysis, separation, and synthetic production of new substances had its reward not only in gaining a satisfactory scientific system but also in a great extension of practical use as dyestuffs, plastics, motor fuels, and in the chemical production of highly specific materials for food and health.

The principle of organic chemistry, that a pure substance is defined by reproducibility in a definite atomic structure of its molecule, had to be maintained against the concepts of oscillations and vibrations developed in physical chemistry. Invasions of these concepts into organic chemistry occurred at various times. The first invasion used a weak spot in the theory that every compound had one definite arrangement of the atoms in its molecule. When Adolf Baeyer, in the continuation of his indigo studies, investigated the chemical reactions of isatin, he found that two structural formulae were indicated for this one compound by its reactions. With acetylating agents, it reacted according to Formula I; with silver and methyl iodide, according to Formula II. Once this exceptional case was established, a search for analogies began. The exception to the old rule could be validated only by being made part of a new rule.

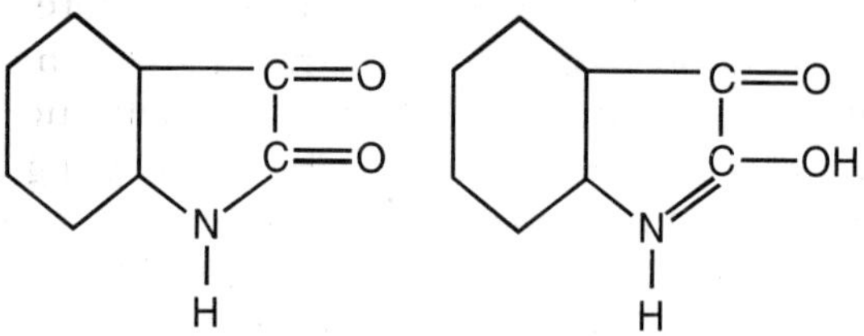

So long as only this particular set of reactions was considered, the structure could be explained as varying with the conditions of the chemical change, following the way which Berzelius had recommended in a similar difficulty. But times had changed. The techniques of separating isomers were finer; the identification by chemical reaction could be amplified by the measurement of physical properties in which the substances were observed without chemical influences and compared with a large group of other substances.

Conrad Laar (1853-1929) tried to develop such a new rule. The configurations

$$\begin{array}{c} -\mathrm{C}=\mathrm{O} \\ | \\ -\mathrm{N}-\mathrm{H} \end{array} \quad \text{and} \quad \begin{array}{c} -\mathrm{C}-\mathrm{OH} \\ \| \\ -\mathrm{N} \end{array} \quad \Bigg| \quad \begin{array}{c} -\mathrm{C}=\mathrm{O} \\ | \\ =\mathrm{C}-\mathrm{H} \end{array} \quad \text{and} \quad \begin{array}{c} -\mathrm{C}-\mathrm{OH} \\ \| \\ =\mathrm{C} \end{array}$$

appeared in other newly discovered compounds. Apparently hydrogen could oscillate between two positions and form pairs of compounds which Laar called ìtautomericî. The models shown above represent the extremes between which the oscillation takes place.

It was first shown for compounds corresponding to Model II that the two forms could be separately identified. Transitions from one form to the other, and equilibria conditions, could be established for them. The principle of definite constitutions was confirmed, the invasion repelled. The victory brought a definite gain to organic chemistry. The rigidity of the concept of molecular structure was cautiously modified. In the pictorial representation of this structure, the lines indicating valence bonds were broken up. Wernerís distinction between primary and auxiliary valences and Thieleís partial valences had their successors in Hugo Kauffmann theory of split valences which gave, for example, the following drawing for phenol:

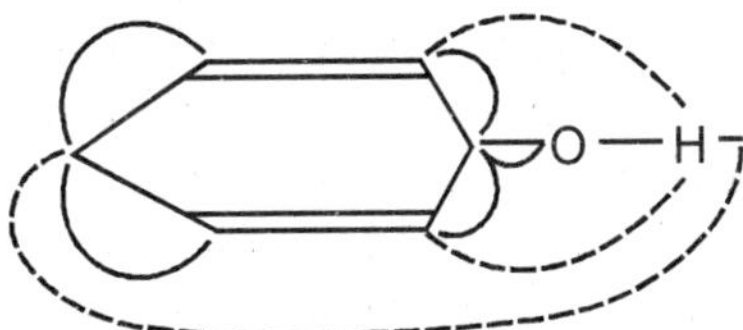

The splitting of the hydrogen valence between oxygen and carbon atoms of the benzene ring was offered as an explanation for the acidity of phenol, which is much greater than the acidity of alcohols without a benzene ring, e.g., C_2H_5OH (ethyl alcohol). Kauffmann further read into his formula the presentation of the influence which the introduction of anóOH group has on the visible color of aromatic compounds.

Carl Graebe and Carl Liebermann had concluded from their studies of quinone and alizarin that ìthe physical property of color depends upon the manner in which oxygen or nitrogen atoms are grouped, that in the colored compounds these elements are in a more intimate bond to each other than in the colourlcss compounds.î A simple example for this rule was azobenzene (Formula I), which is yellow-red. When the ìmore intimateî double bond betweell the two nitrogen atoms is opened by adding hydrogen, colorless hydrazobenzene (II) is formed:

C_6H_5 ñ N = N ñ C_6H_5

(I) Azobenzene

$$C_6H_5 - \underset{\displaystyle H}{\underset{|}{N}} - \underset{\displaystyle H}{\underset{|}{N}} - C_6H_5$$

(II) Hydrazobenzene

Otto N. Witt (1853-915) distributed the color-forming effect over two factors: One was the chromophore for example, nitrogen or nitrogen with oxygen, in the ìmore intimateî double bonds; the other a contributing or enhancing factor, the auxochrome. A hydroxyl group can function as an auxochrome (1876, 1888). The cause of color, which had formerly been seen in the presence of the old colour - giving element sulfur, was now attributed to constituent parts of the molecule and their combined influence. H. Kauffmann (1911) made a further distinction between independent chromophores like the nitroso-group N = O, and dependent chromophores like C = O, which need additional chromophores to be effective. The cumulation of such groups, their intimate neighbourhood, was decisive. Acetone, CH_3 ó CO ó CH $_3$, is colorless; diacetyl CH_3 ñ COó COóCH_3, is yellow; triketopeiitaiie CH_3 óCOóCO-COóCH_3 is orange-red. Benzophenone

is colourless; an additional bond between the two benzene rings produces an orange colour in fluorenone,

The rule was confirmed in many cases but it did not cover all colored compounds adequately. The important group of dyestuffs derived from triphenyl methane was best explained by assuming that

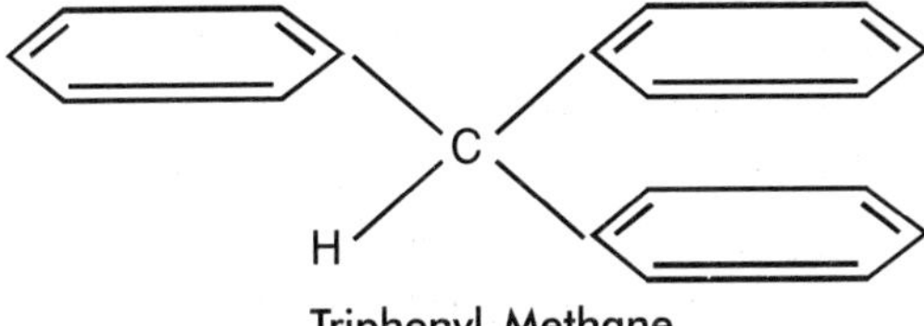

Triphenyl Methane

partial, or split, valences extended between groups which in the older theory would have appeared as separately saturated. The salts of crystal violet were thus represented by a formula with partial valences between the amino groups. In addition, the acid radical X was here seen as bound by the entire basic molecule, not by one specific part of it as the older theory would have prescribed.

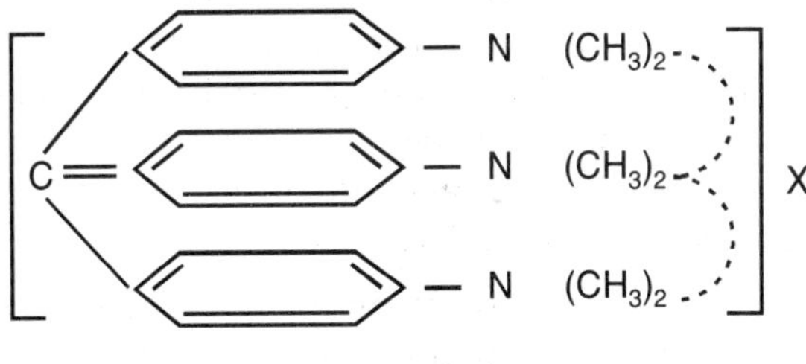

Crystal Violet

Much thinking and a great amount of experimental effort resulted in adding a few small broken lines to the picture by which atomic relations in the molecule of this dyestuff were symbolized. A great deal of chemical history was compressed into such a picture. Its great beauty was not static, and it did not only indicate what this one substance, crystal violet, ìreallyî was, but it also contained the directions for further conclusions. As it was derived from theories and experiences concerning methane, benzene, quinone, substitutions by additional groups and comparisons with other colored substances. it pointed the way to the construction of other dyestuffs. This construction could start on papcr. There was sufficient basis for predicting properties of molecules to be built, and sufficient freedom in expecting and utilizing differences between the predicted and the observed results. Since cumulation of ìintimateî bonds should deepen the color, benzene would be replaced by naphthalene, azo-groups would be multiplied, auxochromes would be introduced.

Such formulations went beyond the ìclassicalî concept that valences are simple and indivisible bonds between the atoms of a molecule. By the end of the nineteenth century, this concept, only about thirty years old at that time, lost its strict validity and became merely an approximation to the truth. New experiences brought other modifications of relatively young theories. Reactions with optically active substances had to be interpreted as showing that the atoms are much freer than previously foreseen to rearrange themselves in the molecule. Compounds in which the quadrivalent carbon atom was only trivalent were discovered. Here were substances of the kind which had been called radicals in the second quarter of the nineteenth century. They had been defined as closely knit parts of a molecule, now they were found to exist in a free state. Concurrently, radicals with a bivalent nitrogen atom were constructed by Heinrich Wieland.

And yet, these new findings enlarged rather than displaced or invalidated the older theories. The physical properties which served to identify these new substances were, as always before, in precise relationship to definite chemical structures. Arthur Hantzsch emphasized this particularly for the optical properties. No chemical change takes place without its optical equivalent, no essential change in optical properties occurs without a corresponding chemical change. When a dyestuff, like congo red, turns blue through the presence of acid, red under the influence of alkali, a change within the molecule must be the cause. This was successfully proved against a physical explanation which started from an apparently logical assumption that the physical change in color must have a physical cause in particle size or surface developments. The chemical explanation of this color change prevailed, just as it had prevailed, about a hundred years before, in the theory of electrochemical phenomena.

Because organic chemists at university laboratories were completely immersed in building their scientific systems, the industrial chemists could construct substances for commercial production. The effect of this development on national economy can be appreciated from the following statistical figures:

German Trade in Indigo

Year	Import	Export
	(In million marks)	
1896	20.7	6.4
1911	0.446	41.8

Value of German Exports in 1912

In million marks	In long	tons
Alizarin	23.64	11,589
Indigo	45.21	24,827
Other tar dyestuffs	133.76	59.696

The scientific investigation of dyestuffs was based on their relationship to many other substances; the industrial production of dyestuffs was connected with increases in coal-tar distillation, in the manufacture of sulfuric acid, nitric acid, and hydrochloric acid, and with the development of equipment and apparatus for producing and packaging on a large scale.

The availability of synthetic dyestuffs had a remarkable influence on the development of medical chemistry. Anatomists used dyestuffs to make tissue preparations more distinguishable under the microscope. Paul Ehrlich learned this technique as a student of medicine. At first, he was less concerned with the chemical constitution of these dyes than with their fixation by the tissues. A pigment becomes a dyestuff when it has an affinity for the material to which it is applied. Acid pigments dye silk and wool, but cotton needs an intermediary, a metal compound which serves as a mordant. Ehrlich was impressed with Paul Schutzenbergerís theory that animal fiber acts like a mordant. The noisonous action of alkaloids had been explained by their elective affinity for protein. Ehrlich felt intuitively that an analogy existed between the chemical combination of alkaloids with living protein and the elective coloring of tissue by dyestuffs (1878). He used methylene blue, which Heinrich Caro had recently (1876) discovered, to stain bacteria and cell nuclei selectively (1881). One day after Robert Koch described (1882) his discovery of the tubercle bacillus, Ehrlich was able to show him an improved method for staining it. Besides elective affinity between tissue and dyestuff, there is also specific chemical action which is caused by the oxygen demand of the living cell. This demand can be great enough to take oxygen out of the dyestuff and to reduce it to its colorless leuko-form. It was known that indophenol blue yielded its oxygen more readily than alizarin blue. Ehrlich used (1885) this known difference as a method for comparing the avidity for oxygen in specific parts of the organism. The reaction in the living body, *in vivo*, occurred with water-insoluble dyestuffs, while reactions in the test tube, *in vitro*, prefer solutions. The old adage that substances do not react unless dissolved was therefore changed by Ehrlich for organic reactions: Substances do not act unless fixed. For this fixation of substances to tissues, he developed a working hypothesis which was too crude and much misunderstood, yet useful in many respects.

In this region of supposed chemical reactions with unknown and certainly complex factors in the organism, the analogies had to be bolder than in a field where scientific data were more closely planted. Since the azo-dyestuff trypan red protected mice against the results of infection by trypanosomes (the microorganisms causing sleeping sickness), Ehrlich concluded that the double-bound nitrogen group in this dyestuff caused the beneficial effect. Arsenic is related to nitrogen in the periodic system. Would the substitution of nitrogen by arsenic have particular effects?

The organic arsenic compound called atoxyl had just (1905) been successfully tested by Paul Uhlenhut against the sickness of chickens caused by spirilla. For humans, atoxyl proved to be too poisonous. This substance, which Ehrlich and Alfred Bertheim proved to be arsanilic acid (aniline substituted by arsenic acid), did not have the analogous azo-like structure which was sought. Ehrlich found it in patient experimentation, to which he was led by an original bold analogy. Compound number 606 in the series of experiments, containing two arsenic atoms with a double bond between them, synthesized first in 1909, was effective against spirilla and against spirochaeta, the protozoa producing syphilis.

Natural Dyestuffs

The success in producing synthetic dyestuffs and in recognizing the chemical structure of alizarin and indigo demonstrated that organic chemistry was on the right path. This had been seriously (questioned at various times during the nineteenth century. Objections were raised against ìthe hairsplitting of the organic chemists,î as William Robert Grove called it, and against the unnatural substances produced for no other apparent purpose than to satisfy the demands of a paper- and desk-chemistry. Such criticism came mostly from the ranks of physicists and physiologists, while organic chemists found that to come closer to nature they had to increase the hairsplitting. The methods had to be more gentle, the separations more delicate in the approach to the chemistry of the two most important natural pigments, the green chlorophyll of plants and the red hemine of blood.

Physical methods had been introduced into chlorophyll research at an early stage. David Brewster described the optical absorption spectrum of his chlorophyll product in 1834. The difference of colour between arterial and venous blood invited spectroscopical investigation. When Claude Bernard observed the action of carbon monoxide on hemoglobin, he measured the displacement of oxygen by the poisonous gas and described the accompanying colour change by the characteristic absorptions in the spectral light.

Chemical reactions with acids and alkalies gave a number of different products from chlorophyll, but their relationships found various interpretations. The blood pigment was converted into crystallized derivatives by treatments with salt and acetic acid. They were certainly not identical with the natural substances.

Instead of strongly reacting chemicals, Armand Gautier used absorbent charcoal in his attempts to separate pure chlorophyll from alcoholic leaf extracts. But charcoal was too strong an absorbent; Michael Tswett replaced it by calcium carbonate which selects the dyestuff more exclusively. The gentle method of selective absorption helped to solve the problem of separating highly sensitive substances without changing them. Chlorophyll is sensitive even to the action of alcohol used apparently as a mere solvent. This was shown by Richard Willstatter. He approached the investigation of chlorophyll with the experiences gained in his work on quinones in Adolf Baeyerís laboratory in Munich. The alkaloid cocaine had been another subject of Willstatterís studies. These led him to a new concept of its chemical structure. A by-product of this scientific work was the partial synthesis of one of the alkaloids which accompany cocaine in nature. It was soon manufactured industrially.

When Willstatter turned from quinones and cocaine to chlorophyll, he improved the conditions under which chlorophyll could be separated. He refined the methods for distribution of the pigment in various solvents, which Gregor Kraus had attempted, and of separating its components by adsorption, which Tswett had used. An enzyme, chlorophyllase, is present in grass and leaves. It causes exchange of the ethyl alcohol, used in laboratory operations as a solvent, for another alcohol, phytol, which forms part of the chlorophyll molecule. ïThe method of our investigation was to arrive at the peculiarities of its constitution, without first isolating and investigating chlorophyll itself, on two ways of degradation, namely, by exploring the two series of derivatives which are produced by the reaction with acids (olive-colored compounds) and with alkalies (chlorophyll-green carbonic acids). Thus by splitting with acid we are able to safeguard that component of chlorophyll which is separated by alkali. On the other hand, the alkali derivatives of the dyestuff must retain a characteristic atom group which is destroyed by acid so easily and with such striking change of colour.î

Magnesium, in an amount of nearly 3 per cent, was established as an important part of the chlorophyll molecule. Magnesium is stable towa4rd alkali, easily removed by acids, and bound not by the carboxyl group but by nitrogen. The nature of this bond was understandable on the basis of Werneris theory of primary and secondary valences. The basic structure of chlorophyll was closely related to that of the red pigment in hemoglobin.

Willstatter published his first report on chlorophyll from the laboratory of the Polytechnicum in Zurich. He continued it with many collaborators in Berlin-Dahlem at the Kaiser

Wilhelm Institute for Chemistry, and in Munich after he became the successor of his old friend and teacher, Adolf Baeyer. In Dahlem he started to include the pigments of flowers and fruits. The materials were harvested from small plantations on the institute grounds, and great care was taken to exclude deterioration between collection and investigation. The new group of dyestuffs, the anthocyanins, showed a uniform principle of structure. Slight chemical changes in the molecule accounted for the great variety of color in flowers. They differ chemically from chlorophyll, and they do not have its important function in the conversion of carbon dioxide and water into carbohydrates, to which Willstatter devoted intensive study.

While there was no doubt that plant colors are due to the presence of chemically definable pigments, it appeared quite uncertain whether enzymes were substances, in the chemical meaning of the word. Enzymes were known by their specific catalytic action. The ìactiveî part of a muscle tissue or a plant juice could be separated from inactive admixtures, but it was enveloped in greater mystery than ìordinaryî chemical substances by its sensitivity to acidity or alkalinity of the medium and heat. Diastase from malt was a widely used enzyme, but was it a substance? Willstatter was convinced that it was. Methods for measuring enzymatic action and concentrating it in a smallest amount of substance, separated from the natural material, gave results which confirmed his conviction. In his book on enzyme studies he reported that enzyme purity could be increased many hundred times compared with the raw materials. The purifications were obtained with silica and alumina, specially prepared with specific adsorptive qualities. James B. Sumnerís discovery of the urea-splitting enzyme ìureaseî from jack beans in crystallized form gave a final confirmation of the chemical concept of enzymes as substances.

The chemistry of the anthocyanins was confirmed and further elaborated by the syntheses which Robert Robinson carried out. At about the same time, the yellow pigments from carrots and lilies were established as belonging to a different group of great biochemical importance, the ìcarotenoids.î Experiences in the field of terpenes, new methods for chemical synthesis by means of magnesium compounds, and improved analytical procedures, were combined with measurements of refraction and absorption of light and with further developments of separation by adsorption. Thus the chemistry of the carotenoids took shape in the 1930ís in work concentrated at the laboratories of Richard Kuhn, Willstatterís former student, in Heidelberg, and in Zurich at the laboratories of Paul Karrer, who had studied under Alfred Werner and had worked with Paul Ehrlich.

The constitution of hemin was cleared up in all details and verified by synthesis by the long work of Hans Fischer in Munich, who died just before he could complete the same for chlorophyll. This purely theoretical work had an unexpected industrial consequence. During the synthetic production of phthalimide by condensation of phthalic anhydride with ammonia in the plants of Scottish Dyes, Ltd., a dark blue ìimpurityî was often formed. The product contained iron from the reaction vessel. The basic information on hemin and chlorophyll made it possible to explore the chemistry of the blue ìimpurityî and to start the development of a new group of synthetic dyestuffs of exceptional stability, the phthalocyanins, a work that has been going on since 1928.

Purines and Proteins

The excretion of uric acid had its physiological origin in proteins. Medical interest in the chemistry of uric acid was as great as the purely chemical one, particularly since an alkaloid, caffein, was closely related to uric acid. Besides, the alkaloid theobromin from cocoa forms caffein by introducing a methyl group, as Liebigís pupil A. F. L. Strecker

(1822-1871) showed in 1861. Transformations by chlorine and methyl substitutions in the molecule of uric acid were the procedures by which Emil Fischer established the structural relationships of these substances. This work, which began in 1882, was complicated by the tautomerism of uric acid.

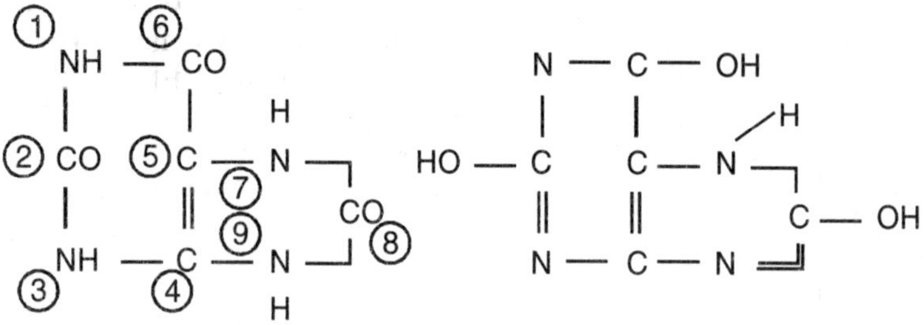

```
(1)      (6)
  NH  —  CO                          N — C — OH
  |      |    H                      |   |   /H
(2)CO  (5)C — N ⌐        HO — C      C — N ⌐
  |      ||(7)   CO                  ||  ||      C — OH
  NH  —  C — N ⌟ (8)                 N — C — N ⌟
(3)     (4)(9)
              H
```

Besides, it proved very difficult to obtain specific reaction in position (8). In 1897 the formula which Ludwig Medicus had anticipated twenty-two years earlier was proved. The methyl group which causes the difference between theobromin and caffein was located in position (1). Caffein without the methyl in position (7), was identified with another alkaloid, theophyllin. Adenin, an alkaloid found in tea extract, could be structurally derived from the tautomeric form of uric acid, with hydrogen in place of its hydroxyls and with an amino group on carbon (6). All these substances could be considered as derivatives of a *purum uricum*, which Fischer called ìpurine.î He finally prepared it by reducing the iodinated uric acid with zinc. The demands of the chemical formulations were met. Pure substances were found which the system of organic chemistry permitted to be formulated on paper. A number of natural products were identified with their position in this system.

All those syteniatic connections appeared at first as purely theoretical but they influenced that other system of facts which is called ìappliedî or ìpractical.î Julius von Mering had expected to obtain a sedative or sleep-inducing substance by attaching methyl groups to urea. Emil Fischer constructed a dietliyl derivative of barbituric acid instead. It was successful as a medicament under the name ìveronalî and, modified by substitution of a phenyl for one of the ethyl groups as ìluminalî.

A few of the products obtained by the hydrolysis of proteins were known by analysis and synthesis. Jacob Volhard Liebigís pupil and later his son-in-law, identified ìsarkosinî (from Greek *sarx* = flesh) by synthesis from chlorinated acetic acid and methylamine (H_2NóCH_3)

```
H
HC — COOH
|
HN — CH3
```

in 1862. Hippuric acid was a benzoyl derivative of aminoacetic acid (glycine), as Victor Dessaignes proved by synthesis in 1853. Theodor Curtius discovered that this synthesis also leads to products of higher condensation. Amino acids can be esterified in the usual reaction with alcohol, containing as a catalyst, hydrochloric acid. This acid combines with the amino group and can be removed by digestion with silver oxide. The method found by Theodor Curtius was delicate and costly. When Emil Fischer substituted sodium hydroxide, under controlled conditions, for the silver oxide, he made it possible to obtain the esters of amino acids quickly and inexpensively. The esters were easily separated in pure form by distillation.

The stereoisomers of the amino acids could not, however, be separated in the usual way. The influence of the basic amino group weakened the acidity of these acids so that they did not form salts with the optically active alkaloids. A preliminary reduction of the influence of the amino group was necessary. It was achieved by introducing acetyl groups in place of hydrogen in the amino group. The separation into the optical antipodes thus became feasible. Optically active alkaloids formed characteristic salts and the optically active amino acids could be recovered from them. Hydrolysis of casein by sulfuric acid of 25 per cent strength, and then with concentrated hydrochloric acid, gave a number of different amino acids, of which Emil Fischer and his callaborators identified and separated 70 per cent. The knowledge of the products of hydrolysis opened the way toward synthesis. In 1907 Fischer succeeded in combining, in a chemically controlled manner, eighteen amino acid fractions to a peptide of molecular weight 1,213. While excited reporters announced that the ìgreatest riddle of lifeî had been solved, Fischer knew and emphasized that no real protein had yet been produced artificially, not even silk fibroin which appeared to be one of the simplest proteins. And while biologists had reasons to doubt that the methods used in the investigations were adequate for the synthesis of a natural protein, Fischerís former pupils continued to explore the relationships between amino acids and the products of their syntheses. Emil Abderhaldencombined chemical with physiological research on the nutritive importance of each amino acid. Max Bergmann extended it in physicochemical directions and applied the methods, particularly to the investigation of hide and leather.

Carbohydrates

One of the pure organic chemical substances which are produced in largest quantities and at low cost is the crystallized sugar, saccharose, from beets and sugar cane. World production of this sugar was 10.8 million tons in 1895, 34.5 million tons in 1935. Prices fluctuated under the influence of taxation and government regulation. From the turn of the century to the First World War, the price per pound was listed between 3.5 to 4.5 cents, including 1,685 cents duty. Great improvement in technical equipment, particularly for cane sugar, kept production increasing after the war despite a drop in price. Consumption of sugar in the United States amounted to about a hundred pounds per person in recent years. Molasses, a by-product of sugar manufacture, formed an important raw material for the production of alcohol by fermentation. Between 1901 and 1926 the quantity of molasses used for alcohol production rose from 14 million to about 240 million gallons. The increase did not continue; influenced by the larger crops of other agricultural products, it declined in some of the later years.

Saccharose is easily hydrolized to the simpler sugars, glucose and fructose. This relationship was not adequately explained by the formula which Rudolf Fittig proposed in 1871:

$$C_6H_7 \begin{cases} O \\ (OH)_4 \end{cases}$$

$$C_6H_7 \begin{cases} O \\ (OH)_4 \\ O \end{cases}$$

This juxtaposition of the two C_6 sugars did not account for the fact that saccharose is a nonreducing sugar. Glucose and fructose reduce alkaline copper or silver solutions, due to the combination of aldehyde and hydroxyl groups. Saccharose does not have a free aldehyde group. Bernhard Tollens therefore suggested in 1883 that the two parts are connected by a carbon-to-carbon bond. A. Wurtz had pointed to this possibility a few years before on the basis of an analogy to ethylene oxide and propylene oxide. A. Colley had formulated glucose with an oxygen bridge between two different carbon atoms:

```
┌─C H2
│ |
│ C HOH
│ |
│ C HOH
O |
│ C HOH
│ |
│ C HOH
│ |
└─C HOH
```

Colley Glucose Formula (1870)

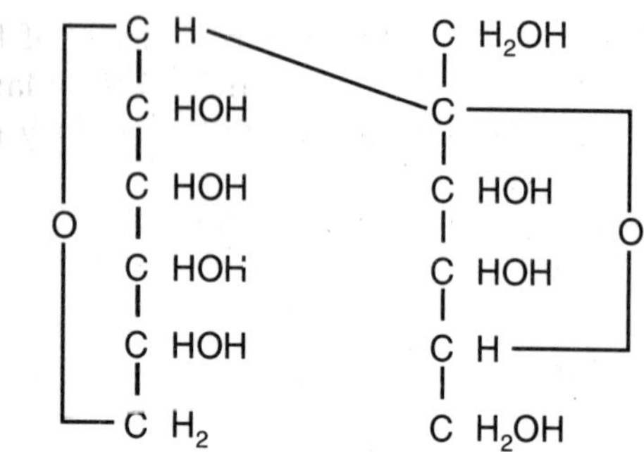

Tollens' Saccharose Formula (1883)

The oxygen bridge could explain why glucose does not readily show all the usual aldehyde reactions. The written formula showed, however, that much of it was still mere conjecture. If there were an oxygen bridge, it could connect any pair of the carbon atoms; and if there were a linkage as shown in the saccharose formula, the ease with which it is separated in hydrolysis would be without analogy. Besides, definite steric arrangements had to be found in order to explain the optical activity of the sugars.

An approach to these problems was facilitated by a new specific reaction which Emil Fischer found. Phenylhydrazine, $C_6 H_5$ ó NH ó NH_2,which he discovered in the course of his work on diazotation, combined with simple sugars and gave crystallizable compounds. This proved to be a reaction by which these sugars could be separated and characterized. Reaction with methyl alcohol under precisely defined conditions gave derivatives which could be separated into optical isomers. The alcohol reacted with the aldehydic oxygen. These compounds, called ìglucosides,î existed in two complimentary asymmetric forms which were distinguishable by enzymes. Definite assignment of the relative positions for the hydrogen and hydroxyl groups around the carbon atoms was the goal. In order to reach it, comparisons between all the known simple sugars were necessary. Reactions like those which Heinrich Kiliani found in oxidation or in combination with prussic acid were used to arrive at a three-dimensional model of the sugars. Projection of the tetrahedral structure on the plane of paper gave the sterical formula for the dextrorotatory glucose:

```
       H
    ①  C═O
       |②
      HC OH
       |③
    HO C H
       |④
     H C OH
       |⑤
     H C OH
       |⑥
     H C OH
       H
```

d—Glucose

Even now the formula was not complete. The oxygen bridge had to be provided. In accordance with Baeyerís strain theory, it was assumed that it combined carbon (1) with carbon (4). The two methyl glucosides were then assigned the following structural formulas:

```
H3C—O—C—H                      H—C—H—CH3
      |  \_______                |\_______
   H—C—OH        |            H—C—OH     |
      |          |               |       |
  HO—C—H         O           HO—C—H      O
      |          |               |       |
   C—C———————————             C—C—————————
      |                          |
   H—C—OH                     H—C—OH
      |                          |
      C—H2OH                     C H2OH
```

Fischer's a—Methyl d-Glucoside   β —Methyl d—Glucoside

Horace S. Isbell and Claude S. Hudson reduced the uncertainties of this model still further. The properties of the acids obtained by oxidation could best be explained with an oxygen bridge linking carbons (1) and (5). The perspective formula of W. N. Haworth gave a truer picture of the glucose molecule.

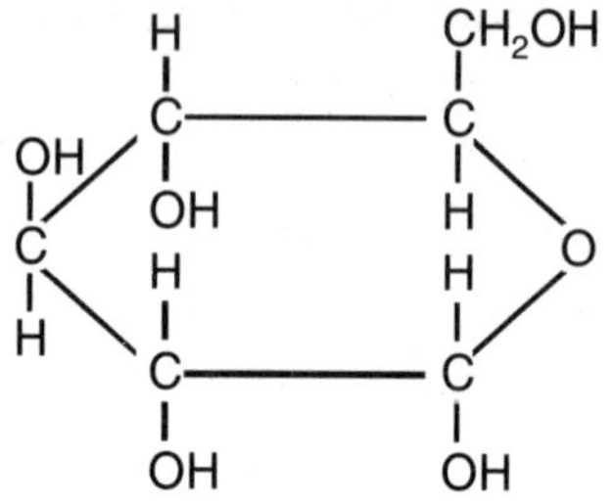

Haworth Glucose Formula

These formulations expressed many relationships between derivatives and the large group of other sugars. The saccharides, which are composed of several simple sugars, offered additional problems.

By complete hydrolysis, starch can be converted into the same simple sugar, glucose, as cellulose. A gradual hydrolysis, however, gives starch in the form of the ìdoubleî sugar, maltose, when cellulose forms cellobiose. The difference between these two bioses was completely explained by Haworth as one of the steric arrangements. The question remained, how many molecules of glucose, or maltose and cellobiose, respectively, were combined in starch and in cellulose.

The question could be formulated because of all the preceding work on molecular structure and the theory of polymerism; the answer could be approached by combining many experimental methods and coordinating their results. Rontgen spectra revealed a crystalline structure in cellulose. The viscosity of dissolved cellulose derivatives, particularly the nitrates and acetates, could be interpreted in its functional indication of the size of the molecules. The rate at which cellulose splits into simple sugars under the influence of dilute acids could be regarded as being related to the degree of polymerization. Purely chemical methods were designed to show whether the glucose molecules were arranged in chains or in rings. A chain has end groups which differ from the links, a ring consists of equal members. Models were built to show mechanically possible molecular structures and to indicate experiments for their verification.

The results for cellulose ruled out early suggestions of low molecular weights and gave figures which increased from a few hundred in the beginning of this research to over a thousand at later stages. Starch, too, proved to be built from a great number of glucose units. LÈon G. M. Maquenne separated starch into two components, ìamyloseî and ìamylopectin,î but the distinction between these components became less strict and universal when starch from various plants was investigated. Plants produce more difference in the kinds of starch than in the cellulose they synthesize.

Synthetic Polymers

The extensive scientific research on high polymers was to a considerable extent supported by a new chemical industry which had its origin in several ingenious discoveries and which needed more basic information as it grew. The first of these discoveries consisted in a mere mixture. In 1868, John Wesley Hyatt found that a nitrocellulose, ìpyroxilin,î acquired greatly improved plastic properties when it was mixed with camphor and a little alcohol. In 1897, W. Krische and A. Spitteler observed that casein can be hardened and made more permanent by a treatment with formaldehyde. Reactions between phenol and formaldehyde, which A. Baeyer had studied in 1878, were found by Leo H. Baekeland to offer great industrial possibilities. He demonstrated molded articles and varnishes prepared from phenol-formaldehyde resins in 1909. At the end of the war in 1918, a large surplus of phenol was on hand. It amounted to over twenty thousand tons. This was soon consumed in manufacturing the new resins for which the expanding production of radio receivers offered a great market.

New sources for synthetic plastics were opened up through condensations of formaldehyde with urea and more recently with melamine or through polymerisation of unsaturated organic compounds like styrene and vinyl derivatives. While the production of plastics from cellulose increased to a maximum of 133.4 million pounds in 1946, the other plastics gradually took a much greater share of the total production of synthetic resins. The same trend can be seen in the development of synthetic fibers. The yearly consumption of textile fibers, in million pounds, grew from 4,715 in 1937 to 5,739 in 1949. The difference of 1,024 million pounds contains 743 of synthetic fibers, or 3.5 times as much in 1949 as in 1937. A large part of the chemically made fibers was produced from the natural polymer, cellulose, but the synthetic polymers increased their share greatly.

Ethereal and Mineral Oils

Ethereal Oils: Turpentine and the oils obtained from plants by steam distillation are composed of carbon and hydrogen. A connection between these ethereal oils and india rubber (caoutchouc) came to light when Charles Greville Williams obtained as a product of its thermal decomposition a low-boiling hydrocarbon which he named ìisopreneî. The chemical formula for this oil, C_5H_8, suggested to Berthelot that it was the simplest type of terpene. The polymerisation of isoprene gave terpenes of the formula $C_{10}H_{16}$, and sesquiterpenes, $C_{15}H_{24}$, built from three molecules of isoprene. Gustave Bouchardat actually produced terpenes from isoprene by heating it, under pressure, to temperatures of 280 C.

When KekulÈ converted the terpene, from which this group of hydrocarbons received its name, into ìcymeneî, he showed that terpene is a benzene derivative with a methyl and an isopropyl group, present, as in cymene, in para position. Menthol, from peppermint leaves, and camphor from the wood of the camphor tree (*Cinnamomum camphora*) are solids at ordinary temperatures, ìcoagulatedî ethereal oils, in the language of the seventeenth century.

KekulÈ found that camphor, a ketone, can be converted into p-cymene (and carvacrol, a derivative of menthol), and he formulated camphor accordingly.

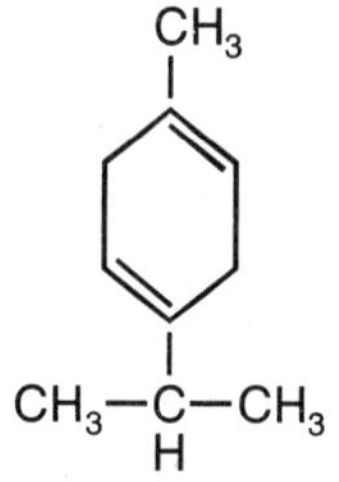

Terpene Kekule

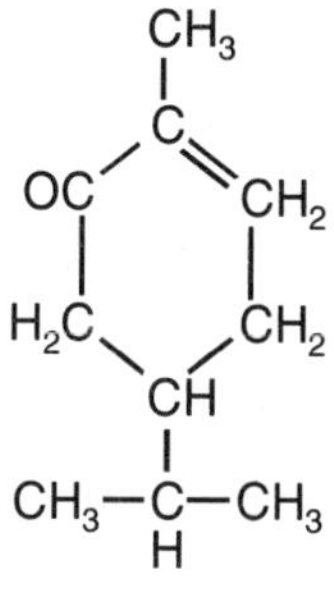

Camphor Kekule

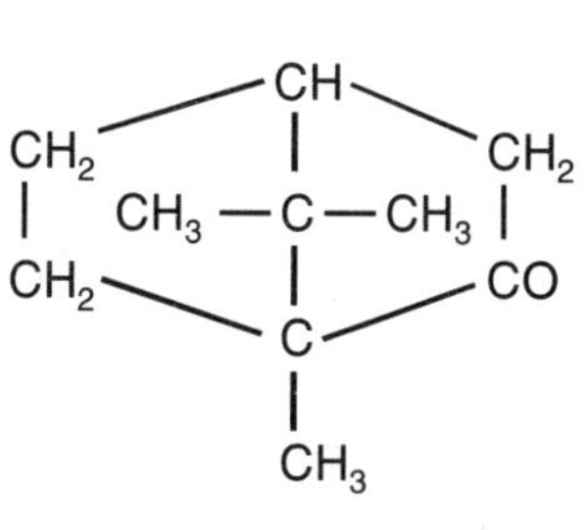

Camphor Bredt

Stepwise oxidation showed, however, that the carbon atoms of the methyl and isopropyl groups were not freely attached to the hydroaromatic ring, but formed a second ring within it. C. Julius Bredt introduced the concept of the bicyclic structure with his camphor formula (1893). Synthesis verified this structure. A synthetic production of camphor had been sought for a long time; Berthelot had produced it from the hydrochloride of pinene, the main constituent of pine oils, by oxidizing the intermediately formed camphene. Scientific and economic interests were combined in these efforts to manufacture a substance on which Japan had a monopoly and which was used in medicine and in the plastics industry.

These dual interests supported each other in the systematic work on terpenes to which Otto Wallach devoted a lifetime of research. Industry needed methods for identifying ethereal oils by the pure substances which could be separated from them. Falsification could thus be detected, new compositions could be produced. A comparison of the new system of ethereal oils with the plants from which they came showed that chemically similar substances could be obtained from botanically different sources. The isoprene rule, which Berthelot had formulated and which Wallach confirmed, found a new and wider application by Leopold Ruzicka. Carotenoids could be considered as consisting of isoprene units, combined in rings and chains. A basic connection between terpenes, natural rubber, sterols, vitamins, and hormones was supplied by this building stone of the large molecules.

Mineral Oils

The chemical substances already mentioned were used for their specific actions on substances or organisms. Mineral oils are chiefly used for their heat value. The increasing part which oils and hydro-carbon gases played in the rising energy requirements can be seen in developed countries.

Simple distillation of crude oils did not furnish enough of the relatively low boiling fraction which could be used for motor fuel. Higher boiling oils were therefore split by treatment at high temperatures. The gaseous hydrocarbons in natural gas were polymerized to yield gasoline.

Boiling point and caloric content were found to be not the only criteria for the suitability of an oil for automotive engines. Performance under these conditions depended upon the chemical structure of the fuel. The natural gases and oils were subjected to chemical reaction, rearrangement of the atoms, addition of side chains by alkylation, isomerization by catalytic processes. Catalysts were also directly added to the gasoline, particularly tetraethyl lead. ìThe single invention, tetraethyl lead, increased the available horse power of the automobile engines made in the year 1941 by an amount equal to 75 Boulder Dams!î

As lubricants, mineral oils were originally regarded as substitutes for vegetable oils. In automobile races, castor oil was the preferred lubricant as late as 1936. Scientific research on lubrication received a new impulse through the expansion of automobile production. Terms like ìunctuousness,î ìoiliness,î ìlubricityî were used to indicate a property which was gradually correlated with the molecular form, viscosity, surface tension, and film strength. Results were rather confusing for a long time. Lubricating oils were compounded with substances which would extend their usefulness over a wide range of temperatures and reduce secondary changes through oxidation. ìThe crankcase oil of the future should be made with the same precision and understanding that metallic alloys are made today.î

11

Hydrogen Element in Chemistry

Introduction

A collection of models of molecules, hypothetical or real, of all the binary hydrogen compounds of the inert-shell and 18-shell elements can be used to demonstrate spectacularly the periodicity of the elements, as well as to help correlate and explain the properties of the hydrogen compounds. I would recommend at least the following: (gaseous molecules where the compound under ordinary conditions is ionic or highly polymeric solid) LiH, BeH_2, B_2H_6, CH_4, NH_3, H_2O, HF, NaH, MgH_2, AlH_3, SiH_4, PH_3, H_2S, HCl, HBr, HI, ZnH_2.

In addition, you will find crystal models of LiH or NaH helpful and also BeH_2 or AlH_3. You may wish also to have models of B_4H_{10}, B_5H_9, and $B_{10}H_{14}$, and perhaps H_2O_2 and N_2H_4.

Prediction of Compounds from Atomic Models

The molecular models of binary hydrogen compounds to your class, you may find it very helpful to begin with the corresponding atomic models and let your students, under your guidance, predict the probable nature of the compounds with hydrogen. From the model of lithium, for example, they can see its capacity to form but one covalent bond, and the similar capacity for hydrogen is noted from the hydrogen model. They can easily predict that the two elements will unite one to one. From the obviously higher electronegativity of hydrogen (yellow-green in contrast to red), they can predict that the bond will be highly polar, the hydrogen withdrawing electron charge from the lithium. They can predict that this should result in expansion of the hydrogen sphere and contraction of the lithium sphere. Now if you show them the model of a single molecule of lithium hydride, they will be pleased and impressed to find it meeting exactly the specifications which they were able to predict from the atomic models alone.

Examination of the atomic model of beryllium will disclose that this atom can form two covalent bonds that these must be located at opposite sides of the atom if the two vacant orbitals are not to be used in the bonding. The students can see that although the electronegativity of beryllium is substantially higher than that of lithium, it is still much less than that of hydrogen. Consequently, they can predict that the bonds to the two hydrogen atoms that will unite with each beryllium atom will be quite polar, but not so much so as in lithium hydride. The expansion of the hydrogen and the contraction of the beryllium can also be predicted. If you will now show them the model of beryllium hydride (gas molecule), they will see its linear shape, the blue-green of the hydrogen and the orange-red of the beryllium, and feel the gratification that comes from successful prediction and a feeling of understanding.

From the model of boron, they can see that it can form three bonds toward the corners of an equilateral triangle about the boron nucleus, and will therefore unite with hydrogen in a one to three ratio. From the boron electronegativity, they can see that the bonds will be less polar than in the beryllium hydride, but still somewhat polar since the hydrogen is clearly more electronegative than the boron. Unless they know about hydridic bridging, discussed below, they will not be able to predict that two BH_3 groups will dimerize and thus each will become nonplanar, using the fourth boron orbital. This they need not be ashamed of, for the best of chemists would not have predicted this either at the time of its discovery. In fact, the dimeric nature of boron hydride gave the theoretical chemists a shock from which they have not yet altogether recovered. But your students will see, when you show them the diborane model, that their predictions about bond polarity and relative numbers of atoms were entirely correct.

A model of a carbon atom will show your students very clearly that it is capable of uniting with four hydrogen atoms, to be located at the corners of a regular tetrahedron around the carbon. They will predict that the bonds will be very close to nonpolaróin fact, from the carbon and hydrogen models, unless their eyes are delicately color sensitive, they may think the electronegativity difference is zero. Actually the carbon should be just a little greener yellow than the hydrogen. Your model of methane will confirm their predictions. The carbon is yellow-green indicating slight negative charge. The partial charge on hydrogen, although positive, is too small to be shown by the colour scale, and the atoms are therefore yellow for nearly neutral.

From a model of a nitrogen atom they will see that although five electrons are available, only three vacancies to accommodate electrons from hydrogen atoms are there. Consequently only three hydrogen atoms can unite from one nitrogen atom. They will easily see that the electronegativity of nitrogen is higher, and therefore will be able to predict that in the compound hydrogen will acquire a partial positive charge, contracting a little, while nitrogen expands a little as the result of its negative charge. Furthermore, noting the extra pair of electrons, judging its availability from the negative charge on the nitrogen, and noting the positive nature of hydrogen, they will be able, if they know about protonic bridging, to predict its possibility here. The model of ammonia, of course, confirms all these predictions.

From the model of fluorine your students can observe its limitation to the forming of one covalent bond and infer that its compound with hydrogen will be one to one. From the very high electronegativity of the fluorine they will guess, and rightly so, that the bond will be very polar, although not at all comparable to the polarity in something like sodium fluoride. Again the model of hydrogen fluoride shows the predictable features, including extra pairs of electrons which, combined with the negative charge on fluorine and the relatively high positive charge on hydrogen, suggest strong protonic bridging which is very characteristic of this compound.

There is no need here to continue in this vein through the rest of the periodic table, but it seemed desirable to emphasize strongly how easily your students will be able to grasp the fundamentals of chemical combination and the nature of compounds when this type of approach to the presentation of chemistry is made.

Physical Properties

With the models of the molecules you can point out that toward elements of lower electronegativity hydrogen acts as oxidizing agent, becoming negative. When it is highly negative, as in combination with the alkali metals, no discrete molecules result, but instead ionic crystals which resemble the lattice of sodium chloride. A model of a crystalline hydride will show that hydrogen in this highly negative state, when placed in the environment of cations, occupies a relatively very large volume. (The size chosen for hydrogen in the models of gaseous molecules is much smaller and actually not intended to be taken literally. The only intent is to show that positively charged hydrogen is smaller and negatively charged hydrogen larger than neutral hydrogen, which is the only form for which a reasonably accurate covalent radius is known. How much smaller or how much larger is not known and therefore only arbitrarily represented in the models.) With less negative hydrogen the compounds are less ionic and tend to solidify, it is believed, through bydridic bridging. This is probably the structure of solid BeH_2. With boron the bridging is limited to a double bridge between two borons such that the expected BH_3 has no stable existence but forms the dimer, B_2H_6. In methane the hydrogen is no longer negative, since carbon is slightly more electronegative than hydrogen. No longer is there appreciable association under ordinary conditions until the hydrogen becomes sufficiently positive, as in NH_3, H_2O, and HF, to produce molecular association through protonic bridging.

The states of aggregation of these binary hydrogen compounds thus largely as usual determine the physical properties. Ionic hydrides are nonvolatile and high melting (or decompose before melting). Volatility increases and lower melting points result with decreased association corresponding to decreased negative charge on hydrogen. Then, as hydrogen becomes partially positive, its ability to form protonic bridges increases, and although ammonia, water, and hydrogen fluoride are very volatile, they are not nearly as volatile or as low melting as would be expected if protonic bridging did not occur. A similar trend is noted going across the periodic table from sodium to chlorine, with certain significant dfferences and exceptions. Like lithium hydride, sodium hydride forms ionic crystals. Magnesium hydride is probably somewhat more ionic than the beryllium compound, but still largely associated through hydridic bridging. Aluminum hydride differs from boron hydride in two significant ways: its hydrogen is more negative, since aluminum is less electronegative than boron, and it has more than one vacant orbital that might be employed in the bydridic bridging. Instead of forming a dimer, aluminum hydride forms a polymeric solid presumably by hydridic bridging using outer d orbitals as well. Silane, SiH_4, has negative hydrogen, in contrast to methane, but is so symmetrical that it is very volatile and shows no evidence of bydridic bridging. In phosphine, PH_3, the hydrogen is believed to be only slightly negative, and instead of available empty orbitals, the phosphorus has an unshared electron pair. Thus there is no possibility of protonic bridging such as occurs in ammonia, and phosphine has much lower melting and boiling points than ammonia. Hydrogen sulfide has slightly positive hydrogen, but it is not sufficiently positive, and the sulfur is not sufficiently negative, nor small enough, for appreciable protonic bridging. The contrast in properties between water and hydrogen sulfide is therefore very striking. In hydrogen chloride the hydrogen is now more positive, but again the chlorine is too large for effective protonic bridging to occur, and the contrast in physical properties between hydrogen fluoride and hydrogen chloride is nearly as striking as between water and hydrogen sulfide.

My interpretation of what I choose to call ìhydridic bridgingî is at present somewhat controversial. Some may doubt that there is any fundamental cause and effect relationship between this kind of bridging and any fancied or real partial negative charge on hydrogen. The empirical relationship cannot be challenged, however, for to the best of my knowledge, no ìhydridic bridgingî is known where the charge on hydrogen would be calculated to be neutral or positive, or where an available orbital on a positively charged atom does not exist. Hydridic bridging seems always to occur when the hydrogen is calculated to bear negative charge and the adjacent atom has positive charge and a vacant orbital. The degree of association of binary hydrogen compounds seems very definitely to be related to, and to increase with, increasing negative charge on hydrogen.

Chemical Properties

Hydrogen in the free state is both an oxidizing and a reducing agent. It oxidizes the alkali metals, for example, and it reduces oxygen, both vigorously. In general, hydrogen follows these principles closely. As it changes from the free or neutral state toward increasing partial negative charge, it loses its oxidizing powers and becomes more and more strongly reducing. As it becomes increasingly positive, its oxidizing powers become enhanced and its reducing power diminishes. Closely related to oxidation-reduction, as stated previously, is electron acceptor-donor interaction. Neutral hydrogen cannot act either as donor or acceptor. Negative hydrogen, however, to the extent that it has acquired control of an electron pair, can act as donor. Positive hydrogen, to the extent that it can ìshake looseî from the pair of electrons that holds it imperfectly, can act as acceptor. Complex as well as simple hydrogen compounds are therefore known. Closely related to donor-acceptor action is, of course, acid-base reaction, of which donor-acceptor action is sometimes classed as a more general category. Negative hydrogen is basic, and positive hydrogen acidic.

Armed with these principles, all one really needs to do to predict the chemical properties of binary hydrogen compounds is to study the molecular models. If these show the hydrogen to be highly negative, the compounds will be easily oxidizable, basic, and can form complex hydrides by acting as donors toward Group IIIA hydrides in which the hydrogen is less negative. Thus, lithium hydride can donate to aluminum hydride to form the important reducing agent, $LiAlH_4$. If the models show the hydrogen to be essentially neutral, the compound can be predicted to be relatively unreactive, as for example, methane. If the hydrogen is positive, the compound will be relatively difficult to oxidize, show some acidic and therefore oxidizing properties, and tend to lose a proton readily, at least to form complex hydrogen compounds by acting as acceptor. For example, HF cannot be oxidized by any chemical agent, is definitely acidic, can oxidize reducing agents such as metals, and can lose its proton to a donor such as ammonia, forming the complex ion, NH_4 +.

The basic properties shown by ammonia and, to a lesser but still important degree, by water arise from the unshared pairs of electrons on the nitrogen and oxygen; these compounds are also acidic by virtue of their positive hydrogen.

If positive hydrogen is oxidizing and negative hydrogen is reducing, small wonder that when they come together, reactioní to liberate hydrogen gas is typical. The familiar reaction of water with metallic hydrides is only a special example of this general type of reaction, and your students can predict that it can happen when any compound of negative hydrogen encounters a compound of positive hydrogen. About the only significant exception seems to be phosphine, whose slightly negative hydrogen does not react in this way, but here a pair of unshared electrons is available to the proton more readily than the pair of electrons associated with the hydrogenóphosphorus bond. In a similar manner, certain ions in which hydrogen is negative, such as hydroxide ion, furnish unshared electron pairs to protons rather than hydrolyze to liberate hydrogen gas.

The above is the chemistry of binary hydrogen in a nutshell, and there are many interesting details which are more complex and perhaps not so easily interpreted. However, it does provide a better basis by far for the consideration of hydrogen compounds as a group than the familiar classification of these compounds as saline and covalent hydrides.

Periodicity of Hydrogen Chemistry

The intermediate electronegativity of hydrogen permits an unusually vivid display of chemical periodicity through the models of its binary compounds. In these the hydrogen ranges from relatively large and greenish-blue in colour, in the alkali metal hydrides, to relatively small and red-orange in color, in hydrogen fluoride. The nature of all the elements that form the expected hydrogen compounds, which includes all the inert-shell and 18-shell elements, is disclosed by the nature of these hydrogen compounds and by the condition not only of the combined hydrogen but also of the other element in the hydrogen compound. Since hydrogen is only intermediate in its oxidizing power, elements made highly positive by reaction with hydrogen must initially have been highly reactive, strongly reducing metals. This is shown in the models of alkali metal hydride gas molecules, in each of which the metal atom is red and the hydrogen greenish-blue. Proceeding to major groups of higher number, the hydrogen approaches neutrality and then becomes increasingly positive, but even in the extreme never so positive as it is negative at the other extreme. The reason for this lies in the fact that although hydrogen is classed as intermediate in electronegativity, it is actually somewhat on the high side; there is less difference in electronegativity between even hydrogen and fluorine than there is between hydrogen and the alkali metals.

The effects of similarities and differences within major groups can also be pointed out in the models, or with their use. For example, the alternations in electronegativity that result when the electronic type of atom, descending a major group, changes from inert-shell to 18-shell is clearly shown. The simplest hydride of boron is dimeric, $B_2 H_6$. Aluminum, being less electronegative than boron and therefore differing more from hydrogen, forms a hydride in which the hydrogen has higher negative charge, giving it a greater tendency to associate through hydridic bridging. Instead of $Al_2 H_6$, a polymer,

$(AlH_3)_x$,

results. This tendency toward further association is probably aided by the larger size of the aluminum and possibly by its ability to use outer *d* orbitals. If gallium, the atoms of which are larger, were to continue the trend, its hydride would be even more closely associated. In fact, however, it appears to be dimeric, Ga_2H_6, more like B_2H_6, although solid polymers are also known. This is consistent with a higher, rather than lower, electronegativity of gallium.

In Group IVA a similar situation exists. Methane, with practically neutral hydrogen, is not spontaneously inflammable nor hydrolyzable. Silane, SiH_4, in which the hydrogen is now appreciably negative, is both spontaneously inflammable and hydrolyzable. Under ordinary conditions, neither oxygen nor water attack germane, GeH_4, which is more like methane. This would not be easy to account for if germanium followed the trend set by carbon and silicon, but its alternation in electronegativity back toward carbon is quite consistent with the observed return toward the properties of methane. The model of GeH_4 shows the hydrogen to be neutral.

Surveying the whole periodic table of binary hydrogen compound models, one can visualize the periodic trends in all directions with great clarity. An advantage of hydrogen compound models over oxygen compound models in this respect is that they cover a wider range of chemical activity. Whereas the oxides go, left to right, from non-oxidizing to oxidizing, the hydrogen compounds go from actively reducing to oxidizing. The hydrogen compounds cover, in fact, a wider range of variation in properties than perhaps any other class of compounds, except the alkyl derivatives of the elements which in some respects are quite similar.

12

Applications of Molecular, Ionic and Crystal Models

Introduction

When all outermost electrons are involved in only three bonds, the planar triangular structure predictable from the atomic models of boron and aluminum and gallium results. Models of BF_3, BCl_3, and $B(CH_3)_3$ are helpful in illustrating this. Inclusion of multiple bonding adds models of nitric acid, NO_3^-, ethylene or other olefins, formate or any other carboxylate ion, SO_3, benzene, borazene, carbonate ion, $COCl_2$, and many others.

To demonstrate the pyramidal structure predictable from atomic models of VA elements, where an unshared electron pair must be taken into account, models of NH_3, NCl_3, NF_3, PCl_3, PBr_3, PH_3, PF_3 and others, are suggested. Inclusion of multiple bonding adds to this list models of such compounds or ions as ClO_3^-, $SO_3^=$, and $SOCl_2$.

The tetrahedral structure indicated by atomic models of carbon and silicon is shown in models of CH_4, SiH_4, CH_3OH,

CCl_4, CF_4, SiF_4, $SiCl_4$, diamond, CH_3F, SiH_3Cl, and any of hundreds more. The inclusion of multiple bonding adds such models as those of H_2SO_4, SO_4 =, $HClO_4$, ClO_4, POF_3, $POCl_3$, and many more. The increase from two or three to four bonds, brought about by coordination, is shown by models of BF_3 $O(CH_3)_2$, BF_3 NH_3, $Be(H_2O)_4$ ++, $Zn(NH_3)_4$ ++, Al_2Cl_6, BH_4 -, AlH_4 -, BF_4 -, and others, which are also tetrahedral.

When all outer electrons are involved in five bonds, the structure is more likely to be triangular bipyramidal, as shown by a model of PCl_5, Fe $(CO)_5$, or AsF_5. But if there are six bonds, many models can be used to illustrate the structure. Examples are SF_6, $Al(H_2O)_6$ +++, SiF_6 =, PF_6-, $Co(NH_3)_6$ +++, and others.

In all these demonstrations, a careful consideration of models of the component atoms, followed by study of the molecular models, should serve to help your students understand clearly that molecular geometry has a relatively simple and logical basis in the structure of the individual atoms.

Polarity and Physical Properties of Compounds

The general principles explaining physical properties of elements were discussed in the preceding chapter. In compounds electronegativity differences add their influence. To the extent of these differences, they make the bonds polar. If oppositely charged atoms of a molecule are both exposed to possible outside contact, then electrostatic attraction between molecules is possible, as the molecules align themselves so that oppositely charged atoms of separate molecules are adjacent. This may result in ionic crystals or in polar covalent solids, but in any case it increases the intermolecular attractions far above any ordinary van der Waals interactions. Consequently, higher crystal energy, higher melting and boiling temperatures, and lower volatility result. Models of individual molecules such as NaCl or $MgCl_2$ will help to illustrate this, especially when shown together with the models of their crystals.

When the bonds are less polar, the molecules may be attracted to one another, but not to the extent of losing their identity as in a NaCl crystal. As a result, the crystal energy is usually much lower, as are the melting and boiling temperatures, and the volatility is higher. Examples are represented by models of such molecules as PCl_3, F_2O, SO_2, AsF_3 and ICl.

If the molecules are symmetrical, on the other hand, so that the positively charged atoms are completely, or nearly, protected from outside contact, then the degree of polarity can exert little influence. Indeed, it may even result in reduced intermolecular attractions if the outermost atoms are all of relatively high negative charge. Examples can be shown by models such as of CF_4, SiF_4, CCl_4, and SF_6.

For many purposes a representation of the outer unshared electron pairs and outer vacant orbital of a molecule is unnecessary. One valuable application of such representation, however, often justifies the extra labor in the construction of the models. This application is to the prediction of the state of aggregation of the compound. An important general principle of chemical combination is that *exterior orbital vacancies tend to become filled*, or at least to become shielded so that they are no longer accessible to outside electrons. *If a model shows both unshared outer electron pairs and unoccupied outer orbitals, the compound may be predicted to condense under ordinary conditions to a crystalline solid.* The only known exceptions are the boron halides, wherein the fourth boron orbital, which would remain unoccupied if boron forms three single covalent bonds to halogen, appears either to participate in the bonding or otherwise to be unable to assist in condensation to larger aggregates.

Conversely, any model in which no exterior vacancies occur represents a molecule which can only unite with other molecules through van der Waals interaction, and the crystals are molecular, much lower melting and more volatile.

In addition, relatively stable and nonvolatile ìgiant moleculesî may result when the formation of all possible single covalent bonds leads, as in SiO_2, to a 3-dimensional network. Such stability may be enhanced by multiple bonding involving electron pairs on oxygen and outer d orbitals on silicon.

Visualization of Chemical Equations

Models can be of great help to students learning about chemical equations for the first time. If they can visualize the molecules involved in a chemical reaction, they will understand much more readily why, for example, the formulas for the common gaseous elements must be written H_2, O_2, N_2, Cl_2, instead of H, O, N, and Cl. They will see what is meant by ìbalancing an equation,î for once they understand that atoms can neither be created nor destroyed in any chemical reaction (excepting nuclear reactions), they will see the necessity of representing the same number of atoms of each element on each side of the equation. They will also understand the logic of reducing such an equation to its simplest terms, numerically.

The burning of hydrogen is a good reaction for which to illustrate the equation by models. You can exhibit one H_2 model, pointing out that hydrogen gas occurs in this form, and since the molecule contains two atoms, no fewer than two atoms can be involved in the reaction. You can exhibit one O_2 model, and point out that here also two atoms are the minimum number that can be involved. Then you can explain that when hydrogen burns in air, the hydrogen combines with oxygen to form water, illustrated by a model of H_2O. If you set these models on the lecture bench in the proper order to represent a chemical equation and write the corresponding equation on the board behind them in its incomplete form, the students can begin to see at once the requirements for the complete reaction. With your guidance they can see first that if the minimum number of oxygen atoms that can be involved is two, because a single oxygen molecule contains two atoms, then at least two H_2O molecules must result. You can then supply a second H_2O model, placing it next to the first one on the bench. Your students can then see that it would be impossible to have two H_2O molecules if four hydrogen atoms were not available, and a single H_2 molecule supplies only two. Therefore two hydrogen molecules are needed, and a second H_2 model can be placed with the reactants on the bench. Now your class can see that the number of hydrogen atoms and of oxygen atoms is the same in reactants as in products. No atoms have been lost or created. The equation is therefore complete, or, as is often said, ìbalanced.î Literally, an equation implies an equality, and if inequality exists there is no equation. For this reason it seems preferable to speak of ìcompletingî rather than of ìbalancingî chemical equations. In a similar manner, you can illustrate by models any chemical reactions for which you have models available. The following are by way of suggestion:

1. $H_2 + O_2 \rightarrow H_2O$
2. $H_2 + Cl_2 \rightarrow HCl$
3. $NaOH\ (Na+ + OH-) + CH_3\,COOH \rightarrow H_2O + CH_3\,COONa$ $(CH_3\,COO- + Na+)$
4. $H_2\,O \rightarrow H_3\,O+ + OH-$
5. $CH_4 + Cl_2 \rightarrow CCl_4 + HCl$
6. $CH_4 + O_2 \rightarrow CO_2 + H_2O$
7. $NH_4 + + OH- \rightarrow NH_3 + H_2O$
8. $NH_4 + + H_2O \rightarrow NH_3 + H_3O+$
9. $HCl + H_2O \rightarrow H_3O+ + Cl-$
10. $NH_3 + HCl \rightarrow NH_4Cl\ (NH_4 + + Cl-)$

You will, of course, wish to point out the convention of using the simplest formula of substances existing as non molecular solids, such as Fe for iron and NaCl for sodium chloride. Also you may wish to point out the inconsistencies of choice of formula for molecular solids, sulfur and white phosphorus normally being indicated merely as S and P although they occur as S_8 and $_4$, but iodine being indicated as I_2, its actual molecular formula. You can reassure your students that these exceptions or inconsistencies are not numerous and, in general, the true molecular formula is used for all compounds that are liquids or gaseous under ordinary conditions.

Oxidation-Reduction

The concept of ìoxidation stateî and ìoxidation numberî has limited usefulness, but it also has serious defects. Molecular models are much needed to show more nearly the true state of affairs. For example, electrons are withdrawn to a greater extent from phosphorus in PF_3 than in PCl_5, yet convention dictates that the oxidation state of phosphorus in the former is only 3 but 5 in the latter. Partial charge representations in models show better the actual condition of the individual combined atoms. The formal oxidation state can ordinarily be deduced from the model by noting the number of electrons involved in the bonding and the direction of the polarity.

In general, electronegativity serves as an active force in chemical reaction, in that the higher the electronegativity, the more strongly the atom attracts electrons of other atoms and therefore the stronger an oxidizing agent it is. Now, even though a highly electronegative atom has formed as many bonds as it is capable of, unless it has acquired substantial negative charge in the process, it has not lost its potential oxidizing power. The compound, or the electronegative atom in the compound, is therefore an oxidizing agent. It is a general principle that *a highly electronegative atom will tend to leave its combination with other atoms from which it has not acquired much charge, in order to join with other atoms that can give up electrons to it more easily.* This point, which accounts for most displacement and double decomposition reactions, will be illustrated in detail in later chapters, but here it should be noted that any model in which an initially highly electronegative atom is only yellow-green to green is at least potentially an oxidizing agent, and will tend to oxidize any element from which it can acquire higher negative charge. As the negative charge on the combined electronegative atom increases, the potential oxidizing power of the compound decreases, to the point that with color blue-green or blue, for the initially highly electronegative atom, oxidizing power no longer characterizes the compound. At the extreme, a negative ion cannot act as oxidizer.

Similarly, the capacity of any atom to act as a reducing agent improves as its negative charge is higher. Consequently, the ease of oxidation of a compound tends to be higher if its initially more electronegative atoms are more negative. At the extreme, a negative ion is a better reducing agent than the same atom with any lesser degree of negative charge.

Donor-Acceptor Action

Donor-acceptor, or more general base-acid reactions are closely related to reducing-oxidizing (ìredoxî) reactions. In general, no atom can act as an electron donor unless unshared electron pairs are available to donate and for a given element this availability tends to improve with increasing positive charge. Other factors contribute and may even dominate, but a good rule of thumb is that if other factors are equal or negligible, a given element will be a better donor the higher its partial negative charge. With positive charge, as on the nitrogen in NF_3, donor ability is nearly or completely lost.

Similarly, acceptor activity always requires available orbitals, but orbitals tend to become more available with higher positive charge. This apparently holds not merely for obviously available *s* and *p* orbitals, but also for outer *d* orbitals.

Thermal Stability

Several factors determine the forces bonding atoms together. In general, thermal stability, or bond strength, appears to increase with increasing bond polarity. One can therefore predict from the models, in a very approximate manner, which compounds are likely to be most stable thermally and which to decompose easily when heated. Heats of formation are of course closely related to thermal stability, being generally higher per equivalent, the more polar the bond and the greater the thermal stability. In any series of binary compounds of the same two elements, in which one exhibits different oxidation states, the heat of formation per equivalent is always higher for the lower positive oxidation state and diminishes with increasing positive oxidation state of the central atom. In a series of chlorides of the same element, for example, the models will show more yellow in the blue, the higher the oxidation state of the other element, corresponding to lower polarity and lower bond energy.

One can also observe a relationship between bond strength and relative sizes of the atoms, or principal quantum levels of the valence shells. Two trends are evident: (1) small atoms form stronger bonds with one another than do larger atoms; (2) atoms similar in size form stronger bonds with one another than atoms not similar in size. Here the models are helpful also in predicting the relative stabilities of different bonds.

13

Chemistry of Halogens and its Implication

Introduction

The chlorine and hydrogen models will show that each atom can form only one covalent bond, and the formula, HCl, is thus predetermined. Its polarity is likewise easily predictable from the electronegativities, as indicated by the blue-green of chlorine and the yellow-green of hydrogen.

The lithium model again makes easy the prediction of a 1:1 formula, and its red color showing very low electronegativity suggests high bond polarity, which the red and blue model of LiCl will confirm.

The beryllium model will indicate not only the $BeCl_2$ formula, but also the expected linear configuration of the molecule. Again, the bond polarities can be predicted to be high although not as high as in LiCl. The BeCl2 model of course has no surprises when the component atoms have first been thoughtfully studied.

In a similar manner, the nature of all the other molecular models can be predicted, except the dimeric quality of AlCl13, which can be discussed in a general treatment of the physical and chemical properties.

Following the general principles established earlier, you can now indicate the relationship between bond polarity and state of aggregation of the chloride. The highly polar bonds will correspond to ionic crystal lattices of high stability. As polarity becomes less, association diminishes. In AlCl3 the empty orbital on the aluminum together with the relatively high chlorine charge and therefore availability of unshared electron pairs for bonding, cause, in liquid and vapor state, dimerization to Al2Cl6. One chlorine atom on each of two aluminum atoms serves as donor to the other aluminum, the two aluminums thus becoming attached through a double chlorine bridge. Doubtless you will wish to point out that this coordination increases the bonding electron pairs around the aluminum from three to four, and consequently changes the geometry from planar to tetrahedral. Some bright student will be likely to ask why a similar dimerization of BCl3 does not occur. You will be able to point out that the boron is not as highly positive as the aluminum in their respective chlorides and that the chlorine is more negative in the aluminum compound and therefore a better donor than the chlorine in BCl3, but this will not explain the gallium halides which are dimeric and the fact that even BF3 is not. You may perhaps suggest that ìback coordination,î which means donation of a pair of electrons not already involved in the single bonding from the chlorine, can possibly occur more readily with the smaller boron atom than with the larger aluminum and gallium atoms, thus utilizing the extra orbital of the boron. But no complete and clear-cut answer appears to be available.

Carbon tetrachloride is very symmetrical so that even with its polar bonds the molecule as a whole is non polar. Intermolecular attractions are therefore relatively low, giving the compound relatively low melting and boiling points. These values are, nevertheless, considerably higher than for Cl2 itself, and you may wish to consider possible reasons for this, with your class.

The notorious instability of NCl3 is not something readily explained from the NCl3 model, except in terms of weaker bonds between atoms of different size plus the very high energy of the N=N bonds formed by its decomposition. However, from here on, through Cl2O and ClF, the diminished intermolecular association corresponds to lower bond polarity as clearly shown by the models.

In a similar way, the physical trend from NaCl to Cl2 can be discussed. If vacant orbitals and unshared electron pairs are indicated on all these models, the condensation to crystalline solids can be predicted better than just from observed geometry and bond polarity. The models of LiCl and NaCl gas molecules, for example, will then show three vacant orbitals on each metal atom and three unshared electron pairs on each chlorine atom. If your students have in mind the general principle that chemical combination tends to continue until all exposed vacancies are utilized in bonding or physically shielded from bonding, they will see why, in addition to the reason of the electrostatic forces, these molecules will tend to condense as they do. Similarly, when they observe that such models as those of CCl4 or ClF show no outer orbital vacancies but only electron pairs, they can understand why these molecules do not condense except weakly as permitted by van der Waals and sometimes dipoledipole interactions. You will find it helpful, indeed, to consider in detail each chloride molecule with respect to its likelihood of intermolecular association or other condensation and with respect to the physical properties that have been observed. You will find that your students cannot-nor can youópredict exactly what these properties will be, but they can at least predict approximately, and any specific physical property can be rationalized in terms of the nature of the component ions or molecules.

Chemically, the general principles stated earlier can be illustrated very well by the properties of binary chlorides. Chlorine which in combining has failed to acquire high negative charge retains its potential ability to do so by breaking loose and attaching to some less electronegative atom. Even so apparently inert a compound as carbon tetrachloride, in which the chlorine can be seen to be only slightly negative, can react explosively with finely divided metals if the reaction is initiated. At elevated temperatures carbon tetrachloride is an effective chlorinating agent. With increasing negative charge, however, the combined chlorine naturally loses electronegativity, and all compounds wherein the chlorine of the models is blue-green or blue are relatively inert and ineffective as chlorinating agents.

Displacement and double decomposition reactions involving chlorides can be explained quite well by use of the models, for these involve the important general principle that highly electronegative elements tend to become as negative as possible and that reactions tend to proceed spontaneously or exothermically in the direction of forming the most polar bond possible. Your students can see from the models that if a given element would, by forming a chloride, give to the chlorine a lower negative charge than would be supplied by some other element, the first element is certainly not expected to displace the second from its chloride. The converse is true, and any element that forms a chloride in which the chlorine is more negative will displace from its chloride another element which gives electrons to the chlorine less completely. Double decompositions are similarly explained. For example, the lithium-chlorine bond is more polar than aluminum-chlorine or lithium-hydrogen. When lithium hydride and aluminium chloride are warmed together, a double decomposition (metathetical) reaction could result in aluminium hydride and lithium chloride. One would predict essentially no reverse reaction.

Another general principle is that of donor ability increasing with negative charge acquired. Chlorine in the less polar chlorides has essentially no donor ability, despite its unshared electron pairs. However, chloride ion, or even chlorine only as negative as in aluminium chloride as discussed earlier, can act as donor in formation of many complex compounds. Where less polar chlorides have available outer orbitals, they may become joined to polar chlorides, forming, for example, PCl6-, SnCl6, and so on. Large numbers of such complex chlorides are known. They are analogous to the complex oxides in that the more electronegative of the two other elements becomes part of the anion, leaving the other element as the cation.

Fluorine

Fluorine is the most electronegative element, and consequently all models of fluorides will show the fluorine as having partial negative charge, You may find it helpful to have a set of fluoride models corresponding to your set of chloride models, for a comparison of the two sets will show very well the similarities as well as the effects of the higher electronegativity of fluorine.

The procedure of beginning with atomic models can be followed here. Thus the hydrogen model and the fluorine model will permit the students to predict without hesitation a formula of HF, and that this molecule will be quite polar, with hydrogen positive and fluorine negative. A model of HF will show that the prediction is correct. In a similar manner, just as described in detail for oxygen and hydrogen compounds in preceding chapters, the formulas and molecular structures for other fluorides can be predicted from the atomic models and verified by demonstration of the molecular models. The relationships between the simple molecules and the states of aggregation, and thus the physical properties of fluorides, will all be shown by the models. The chemistry of the fluorides closely resembles that of the chlorides, and therefore will not be covered completely here.

First, the protonic bridging of hydrogen fluoride is of interest. From the model of HF, especially if it includes the three unshared electron pairs of the fluorine, one can see that with the high negative charge on the small fluorine atom and the high positive charge on the hydrogen, conditions are optimum for the formation of hydrogen bonds. It is not surprising, therefore, that protonic bridging occurs in hydrogen fluoride, even in the vapour state at ordinary temperatures, causing polymerization to linear, and possibly cyclic, structures of significant but not high stability. The physical properties of hydrogen fluoride, as influenced by this high degree of association not observed in the other hydrogen halides, are therefore different from those other halides to a degree that is noteworthy, and has led to classification of hydrogen fluoride as anomalous. Thus, hydrogen fluoride has a much higher boiling point (nearly 20) than would be expected from the low values for the other hydrogen halides. In general, it differs from the other hydrogen halides in much the same way and for much the same reasons as does ammonia from other group IIIA hydrogen compounds and water from the gaseous hydrogen sulfide, selenide, and telluride. You may wish to point out that this high attraction between proton and fluoride ion, as shown by the stability of HF and the extent of protonic bridging, results in weakness of aqueous solutions of hydrogen fluoride (hydrofluoric acid) as an acid.

A model of the bifluoride ion, FHF-, will show that the hydrogen is equally distant from each fluorine, an observation interpreted as meaning that the two bonds must be exactly equivalent. In other words, here is not the usual ìhydrogen bondî in which the proton remains attached to its original molecule and remains at a considerably greater distance from the atom of the second molecule that attracts it. Here seems to be truly divalent hydrogen, and as the model shows, if the electronegativity becomes equalized by distribution of the charge among the three component atoms in accordance with their relative initial electronegativities, the hydrogen does not even remain positive, but bears a small negative charge. The bond energy is found to be four or five times as great as that of an ordinary protonic bridge, another important bit of evidence that the bonding here is quite unusual.

Boron trifluoride is interesting in its physical properties, as, although the individual bonds are quite polar, it is a gas with no evidence of the kind of association that makes aluminum fluoride a nonvolatile, high melting solid. The bond lengths are somewhat shorter even than would be calculated from the polarity, and very possibly the extra orbital of the boron is employed to use otherwise unshared electrons of the three fluorine atoms in a partial multiple bonding which thus leaves little opportunity for intermolecular association. However, such use of the fourth boron orbital does not prevent its use in the forming of coordination compounds, boron trifluoride being strongly acidic, acting as electron acceptor in many stable complexes.

A model of nitrogen fluoride will show the bonds to be somewhat polar, with the nitrogen end positive and the fluorines negative, and one would expect from the pyramidal structure that the molecular dipole moment would be quite high. On the contrary, it is quite low, and one may suppose that the unshared electron pair on the nitrogen is caused to adjust its average position in such a way as to counteract much of the polarity induced by the fluorines. However, this electron pair certainly does not thereby become more available for the formation of coordination bonds. With the positive charge on nitrogen, one would expect these electrons to be less availableóthe nitrogen to be a much poorer donoró and indeed it is. Nitrogen trifluoride appears to lack almost completely the basic properties shown by ammonia and amines.

Sulfur hexafluoride is an interesting compound to show by model. In it, none of the fluorine atoms have succeeded in acquiring much negative charge, and hence, in principle, the compound should be a powerful fluorinating agent. Actually, it is amazingly inert. There seems to be no question about the potential for high chemical reactivity being present, but here is a good example of how the lack of a reasonably available mechanism for a reaction results in a seeming inertness. The molecule is highly symmetrical, and the sulfur is so thoroughly shielded from the outside world that under ordinary conditions no outside reagent can attack it. All such a reagent ìseesî when it approaches the SF6 is the unreactive sides of fluorine atoms; the bonds themselves appear to be completely protected.

Across the periodic table, the fluorides vary in much the same way as do the oxides and the chlorides. At the left, the compounds are ionic crystals, ordinarily very stable, high melting, low in volatility. The fluorine, being already negative, has no tendency to become more so, and the fluorides in this region are non oxidizing (not fluorinating agents). Fluoride ion can serve as electron donor, and there are large numbers of complex fluorides and related compounds. Then proceeding toward the right-hand side of the periodic table, one observes that the fluorinating ability begins and increases, that the electron donor activity of the combined fluorine decreases, that as the bond polarity decreases, the strength of association decreases and the volatility increases, with lower melting and boiling points resulting. In short, a collection of models of binary fluorides across the periodic table can show the principles and trends of chemical periodicity very well.

Bromides and Iodides

These compounds resemble the fluorides and chlorides quite closely, so that discussion of them individually should not be needed here. In general, the trends in oxidizing power increasing from iodine to fluorine, and in reducing power increasing from fluoride to iodide, must be taken into account in any comparison among the different binary compounds of halogen.

❒❒❒

14

Oxides and Reactions in Chemistry

Introduction

Beginning with lithium oxide, if you show the lithium atomic model and the oxygen atomic model, your students will be struck at once by the great contrast in appearance. The large lithium atom, with only three electrons, is remarkably larger than the much more compact oxygen atom with eight electrons. As previously pointed out, this difference in compactness is closely associated with the difference in the ability of these two atoms to attract electrons. The very low electronegativity of lithium is represented by the red color and the high electronegativity of oxygen by its greenish-blue color. From the outer electronic configurations of the two, your students can see that one oxygen atom can unite with two lithium atoms, establishing the formula as Li_2O. The high polarity which would be predicted from the models suggests that this substance should not exist as separate molecules, but must be highly condensed in crystalline form. You may not wish to try to provide crystal models of all the solid oxides, but you will find it helpful to have type models and also ìatom-pairî models. The latter consist simply of two atomic spheres, in this case, one of lithium and one of oxygen, showing by relative size and color the calculated covalent radii and partial charge in Li_2O. These spheres are attached not in contact but through a bar of some kindóa wooden stick for the larger models, a piece of pipe cleaner for the smallest scale indicating that this pair is intended to show only the individual atoms of the compound and not the state of aggregation. It is helpful to represent outer electrons and vacancies on these spheres, in the amount that would be left uninvolved in simple covalence. In the lithium oxide the lithium sphere would have three pairs of black balls appended to the surface to represent three vacant orbitals. The oxygen sphere would have two pairs of white balls attached to represent two electron pairs left over after normal covalence. The presence of both vacant orbitals and otherwise unshared electrons thus serves as a basis for predicting a crystalline aggregate of a highly polar nature, since individual molecules would condense rapidly when possessed of these qualities.

The exact nature of this crystalline aggregate can be described with the help of a model of fluorite, CaF_2. Li_2O has the fluorite structure in reverseósometimes called the ìantifluoriteî structureóin which the lithium atoms occupy the positions of the fluorine and the oxygen atoms occupy the positions of the calcium.

The atomic model of beryllium shows that beryllium atoms can form two bonds, and since the oxygen model shows that oxygen also can form two bonds, an empirical formula of BeO can be predicted. The redorange color of the beryllium shows it to have higher electronegativity than lithium but still relatively low, especially compared with the greenish-blue of oxygen. A highly polar type of bonding is therefore easily predictable. An ìatom-pairî model of BeO will serve to verify these predictions, and, by showing two empty orbitals on the beryllium and two pairs of otherwise unshared electrons on the oxygen, suggests very strongly that the state of aggregation will be that of a crystalline solid. A model of wurtzite (ZnS) will serve to illustrate the structure of beryllium oxide crystal, in which each beryllium is surrounded tetrahedrally by four oxygen atoms, and each oxygen by four berylliums. Evidently all four orbitals of the beryllium and all outer electrons of the oxygen are effectively occupied in the crystal bonding.

Boron atoms, as shown by the model, have three outermost electrons and can form three covalent bonds. The formula B_2O_3 is therefore predictable. The state of aggregation is not so evident; however, the presence of a fourth unoccupied orbital on the boron after three single bonds are formed suggests that this orbital might assist in any condensation which might occur. Actually boric oxide appears to consist of a boron-oxygen network, or giant molecule type of crystal. Certainly one could predict considerable polarity in the individual bonds, from the contrast between the yellow-orange of the boron and the greenish-blue of the oxygen.

Molecular oxides begin with the next element, carbon. Here the atomic models would suggest that carbon might unite with oxygen to form a giant molecule network of single bonds, each moderately polar, judging from the initial electronegativities. Instead, greater stability appears to result when two double bonds per carbon atom are formed. Carbon dioxide molecules appear to have bonds of essentially this nature. If all the carbon valence electrons are used in the bonding, and only two bonds are formed, then, as previously generalized, these two bonds must be as far apart from one another as possible. This prediction is borne out by the model of carbon dioxide molecule, which is linear, and shows the predicted polarity of bonds and the bond multiplicity.

From the atomic model of nitrogen and that of oxygen, the only directly predictable formula would be N_2O_3. Actually this compound is quite unstable, decomposing to NO and NO_2 very easily. The latter two are not directly predictable from the atomic models, and neither is N_2O, or, for that matter, N_2O_5. The last named seems to exist in the crystalline state as nitronium nitrate, NO_2 +NO_3-, but its easy volatility suggests that the ionic lattice energy must be very low. Your students can, however, predict that in none of these compounds would bond polarity be very great, because nitrogen is too near oxygen in electronegativity. In all, some partial positive charge must be assignable to nitrogen. Models of all the oxides of nitrogen should be instructive, and especially the model of N_2O_5 for comparison with other models in considering the periodic changes in the chemistry of oxygen as described in a later section. The structure of a gaseous molecule of this oxide should be predictable, for if your students assume, probably correctly, that all outermost electrons of each nitrogen are used in the bonding, then the three bonds formed by each nitrogen atom must be in the same plane with the nitrogen nucleus. One oxygen atom must be shared by two nitrogen, which implies two single bonds here at an angle approximating 100 . The bond angle between the two unshared oxygen atoms on each nitrogen must be somewhat greater than the angle between one of them and the shared oxygen atom, because the former bonds have multiplicity. The model of this molecule will show the predictable structure.

The combination of fluorine and oxygen can also be predicted by your students quite accurately. They will note that since fluorine in the atomic model has the capacity to form but one covalent bond, and oxygen two, the formula should be F_2O. However, they will also note that here is a situation where oxygen encounters an element more electronegative even than itself. Consequently, they can predict a small polarity with oxygen positive, and fluorine negative, and they can understand that this is not actually an ìoxide,î but rather, a fluoride, whose formula more conventionally should be written OF_2. The bond angle, a little less than tetrahedral, suggests that the two lone pairs of electrons on the oxygen may repel one another most strongly of the four pairs, thus forcing the two fluorine bonds a little closer together. The model of this molecule will confirm their predictions.

With sodium again, the capacity to form covalent bonds is one and the electronegativity is very low, as shown by the atomic model. You may be somewhat hard put, then, to explain why when sodium is burned in air or oxygen, the chief product is Na_2O_2 instead of Na_2O. However, you can point out at least that Na_2O is also an oxide of sodium and has the properties of high polarity and condensing to a crystalline aggregate which one could predict from the atomic models. By way of apologizing for natureís seeming incongruity in the normal peroxide formation, you can observe that an electron is lost from a sodium atom with somewhat greater ease than from lithium, and that if each of two oxygen atoms could acquire an electron from a sodium atom without the need of breaking the single bond portion of their bonding, this might happen more easily. Furthermore, the crystal energy of a peroxide so formed of sodium might happen to be considerably greater than of lithium, owing to the larger size of the sodium atoms.

An atomic model of magnesium shows it to be more electronegative than sodium but less so than beryllium, and the prediction of the formula, MgO, is quite straightforward. So, also, is the high polarity of the bonds. An ìatom-pair model will show, as in the case of beryllium oxide, two vacant orbitals on the magnesium, and a prediction of condensation is therefore in order. The crystal structure is not the same, however, for with the larger magnesium and greater polarity comes 6:6 instead of 4:4 coordination. In other words, each magnesium is surrounded by six oxygen atoms and each oxygen by six magnesiums instead of each by four as in beryllium oxide. This is the ìrock saltî structure typical of the alkali metal halides.

Aluminum, as shown by the atomic model, is more electronegative than magnesium, but still should form quite polar bonds with oxygen. In fact, you may wish to point out that the stability of such bonds contributes notably to the success of the thermite process, in which a less polar oxide such as of iron or chromium has its oxygen ìwrenched awayî. by metallic aluminum, with the evolution of a large amount of energy signifying the greater stability of the new bonds. The formula Al2O3 can easily be predicted, and an ìatom-pairî model will show the possibility of the fourth orbital of the aluminum becoming involved in condensation to a crystalline lattice. Here a stable network of aluminum and oxygen atoms is formed, in which each aluminum is surrounded by six oxygen and each oxygen is surrounded by four aluminums. This resembles a rock-salt structure in which one third of the six aluminums that should surround each oxygen are missing from the lattice, in symmetrically located positions.

The atomic model of silicon will show it to be substantially less electronegative than carbon, and consequently capable of forming more polar bonds to oxygen. This, coupled with the lesser ability of silicon to form ordinary multiple bonds, results in a ìgiant moleculeî type of condensation, instead of single molecules of SiO_2 like those of carbon dioxide.

The phosphorus model shows only four orbitals, one of which contains an electron pair and is therefore unavailable for ordinary covalence. One could then predict the formula P_2O_3 and that the bonds would be somewhat polar, with phosphorus positive. It would not be possible, however, to predict the molecular structure, except to observe that the three bonds formed by a phosphorus atom are directed toward the base of a low pyramid. You can, if you wish, begin with a model of P_4, and point out how oxygen atoms could become attached to the edges of the regular tetrahedron of phosphorus atoms, since the bonds in the latter are compressed into angles of presumably high strain. Instead of each phosphorus atom forming three bonds to other phosphorus atoms, with bond angles only 60 , it can, with the help of oxygen bridging, remain in connection with the other phosphorus atoms yet with more reasonable bond angles more nearly tetrahedral. Oxygen bridges on each edge of the tetrahedron would require six oxygen atoms and a separation of the phosphorus atoms from one another to make room for the oxygens. The model of the molecule, P_4O_6, will show the nature of this combination.

Invisible on the phosphorus atom model, however, are the outer *d* orbitals. These must be considered to explain the fact that P_4O_6 molecules can acquire extra oxygen atoms, one on each corner phosphorus atom. The explanation that these additional oxygens are attached by a coordinate covalent bond, the phosphorus electron pair joining with the vacant orbital available on an oxygen atom, is incorrect, as shown by the experimental observation that the bond is very short, much shorter than expected for a single covalent bond. Utilization of an outer *d* orbital of the phosphorus, on the other hand, could permit double bonding to the oxygen, with resultant bond shortening. A model of P_4O_{10} shows the result, and helps the students see why iP_2O_5î is incorrect.

To explain the common sulfur oxides, too, outer *d* orbitals must be invoked. If any of you can think of a good way to represent these orbitals in an atomic model, please let me know. For the present discussion your students will have to imagine them. As they view the sulfur atomic model, they must keep in mind that each of the two electron pairs left after the expected divalence is shown, may produce further bonding capacity by promotion of one electron out of the pair into an outer d orbital. This creates capacity for two new bonds at a time. Thus sulfur can form two single bonds or four or six, but not ordinarily three or five.

Sulfur with oxygen then might most directly (assuming no S-S bonds) form SO, SO_2, or SO_3. Early reports of SO appear unconfirmed, and at present it may be regarded as unknown. Efforts to avoid expanding the ìvalence octetî have led to statements that SO_2 is a ìresonance hybridî of

:Ö—S̈=Ö:

And

$$:\ddot{O}=\ddot{S}-\underset{\cdot\cdot}{\ddot{O}}:$$

However, sulfur can certainly ìexceed the octet,î as in SF_4 for example, and there seems to be no good reason to suppose it does not do so in SO_2. In fact, the bonds are short enough to be double bonds. Similarly, SO_3 seems more reasonably described as having three double bonds, whose length incidentally is the same as in SO_2.

The higher oxides of chlorine likewise require either use of *d* orbitals for double bonding or that the electron pairs of the chlorine be donated to the oxygen. The former seems more reasonable. A model of Cl_2O_7 can be shown as an example of a compound in which, as in SO_3, all outer electrons of a nonmetallic atom are used in bonding by aid of the outer d orbitals.

If you now go back over these models representing the oxides and let the students suggest the physical properties that might well result from these structures, you should find them beginning to understand some of the simpler relationships. They will probably be able to predict relatively strong forces among the atoms in the more polar oxides and recognize that such forces will contribute to relatively high melting points and low volatility. They will be able to study those aggregates which present to their neighbors an exterior of electron pairs only, and thus can have mainly vander Waals type attractive interactions. These they should recognize as leading to relatively low melting temperatures and high volatility. They will probably notice then that the physical differences between nonmetal oxides and metal oxides originate very logically with the differences in nature between nonmetal and metal atoms.

Acid-Base Properties

One of the most important distinctions between metal oxides and nonmetal oxides has been that the former are basic and the latter, acidic. With the help of models, your students can understand what this means and why it should be so.

Let us consider first aqueous systems. Water, as previously discussed and as evident among the models, is intermediate among the oxides in the charge on oxygen, and it can act as electron donor through the unshared electron pairs on the oxygen. It can also act as electron acceptor, through losing a proton to some donor. Water is thus amphoteric. Oxides having more negative oxygen than water can take a proton from water, leaving the hydroxide ion, which is now a better donor and can add to the oxide.

For example, the oxygen in CaO is more negative than the oxygen in water (show the models), permitting a proton to be drawn from the water. The hydroxide ion then donates an electron pair to the positive calcium:

$CaO + H_2O \rightarrow CAOH+ + OH-$

$CaOH+ + OH- \rightarrow Ca(OH)_2$

We call this particular product ìcalcium hydroxide,î but it is only one of a class of complex oxides. In such oxides combination of an oxide of a less electronegative element with an oxide of a more electronegative element results in a complex with the more electronegative element now part of the anion, the less electronegative element the cation. Here hydrogen is the more electronegative and becomes part of the complex anion, OH-.

Water is also the oxide of a less electronegative element compared to most of the nonmetals. In combination with the oxide of an element more electronegative than hydrogen, water oxygen acts as donor, adding to the other element, again forming a complex oxide, but here the hydrogen is the cationic portion, and the other element is in the anion. For example:

$H_2O + SO_3 \rightarrow H_2SO_4$

Now, when water has already lost a proton to an oxide, forming a hydroxide, it is unlikely to be very able to take the proton back again. This would be required of water if the hydroxide were to have acidic properties in aqueous solution. On the other hand, if the hydroxide could coordinate hydroxide ions from water, this would have the effect of leaving behind hydronium ions and thus giving acidity to the solution.

Thus oxides of elements less electronegative than hydrogen can at most be slightly acidic in their aqueous reaction. However, if the element is much less electronegative than hydrogen, its electrons must be largely removed by the OH oxygen, making the bonds very polar and the separation of OH- ions easy. These hydroxides are therefore basic, and the more so, the more polar the E-OH bonds.

But when water acts as electron donor, its oxygen loses some of the electrons it did control to the element that is more electronegative than hydrogen. Consequently the oxygen becomes more electronegative than it was in water, and withdraws more charge from the hydrogen than it did in water. The H-O bond is more polar, and it becomes easier for other water molecules to remove a proton than when the proton was part of water. In other words, the complex oxide is acidic in water solution. And since, as you can easily demonstrate in the models of the free acids such as HNO_3 and H_2SO_4, the bond between oxygen and the other element is less polar than in water, the chance of separation of a hydroxide ion diminishes to practically zero.

The chief reason for the importance of the position of water in the oxide system, however, is that it is liquid and a common solvent. Fundamentally, there is no difference between complex oxides formed by water and those formed by non-hydrogen oxides. For in general oxygen of higher negative charge can act as donor to oxides in which the oxygen has lower negative charge, forming complexes with the more electronegative other element centered in the complex anion and the less electronegative other element cationic. In these terms basic hydroxides, oxyacids, and oxysalts differ mainly in nomenclature. For example, ZnO, which forms an amphoteric hydroxide in water, is amphoteric on its own account:

$ZnO + SO_3 \rightarrow ZnSO_4$

$ZnO + Na_2O \rightarrow Na_2 ZnO_2$

Highly polar oxides can react with slightly polar oxides in only one way:

$CaO + SO_3 \rightarrow CaSO_4$

From the models your students can easily predict the nature of the reaction between metal oxide and nonmetal oxide to form salts. They will then find it easy to understand why the more oxygen that compete for the same electrons, the less negative charge each can acquire and therefore the less basic and the more acidic the oxide is. Models of SO_2 and SO_3 unfortunately will not show this well because the charge on oxygen does not differ sufficiently to show on the color scale. However, a comparison of CrO and CrO_3, for example, will illustrate this trend.

The stability of the complex oxides appears to depend largely on the extent to which the anion can control the bonding electrons without being distorted. If the proton with its high electronegativity and high polarizing power is the cationic part of the salt, it is likely to be relatively unstable. This is shown by the common phenomenon of free acids decomposing more readily than many of their salts, some, like carbonic acid, even being unknown in isolated form. With a model of a hydrated cation you can demonstrate how the anion is protected by the hydration from the charge and polarizing power of the cation. This explains why hydrated salts of oxyanions are more plentiful than the anhydrous salts.

The structure of a typical complex oxide can profitably be shown, because the concept of alternating cations and anions leads to misunderstanding of the real situation. If, for example, you have a crystal model of $CaCO_3$, you can point out that actually each Ca is surrounded by six oxygen atoms, and each oxygen is attached to two calciums as well as to a carbon.

Oxidizing Properties

The oxygen in any oxide can be caused to unite under the right conditions with a reducing agent such as hydrogen, but this does not mean that the oxide is necessarily classified as an oxidizing agent. Under ordinary conditions if the combined oxygen has a reasonably high negative charge, the oxide is not an oxidizing agent. As the negative charge diminishes, however, the oxidizing powers increase. All oxides in which the oxygen is not highly negative are therefore at least potentially oxidizing agents. Study of the models will disclose which compounds these are. Compounds like Cl_2O_7, in which the oxygen has scarcely any negative charge, are naturally stronger oxidizing agents than oxides like carbon dioxide, but the yellowish-green color of the oxygen even here will suggest that carbon dioxide is potentially an oxidizing agent. Indeed, its use to extinguish fires is quite in contrast with the fact that actually the most reactive of organometallic compounds are spontaneously inflammable in carbon dioxide.

Periodicity of Binary Oxygen Compounds

Models of oxides across the periodic table can serve very well to solidify your studentsí concepts of the meaning of chemical periodicity. In such a collection of models, the intermediate position of water is quite clear. They can see at once that in a period, such as from lithium to fluorine, the condition of combined oxygen changes steadily, becoming less negative from left to right. Associated with this change, they will recognize the trend from stable, solid crystalline oxides to volatile, less stable covalent oxides of much lower polarity. The trend is also from strongly basic to strongly acidic oxide, from non reducing to strongly oxidizing compounds. Not only the trends across periods but also the similarities and occasional differences within major groups of the periodic table are clearly evident from the models and an understanding of what they represent. A collection of models of oxides over the periodic table can do much to demonstrate the importance and the real meaning of the periodic law. When your students begin to acquire the fundamental understanding of oxygen chemistry that is so much more easily available with the help of such models, they will be well on their way to developing an understanding and appreciation of chemistry in general.

❑❑❑

15

Model Construction in Chemistry

Introduction

Considerably more expensive and requiring greater storage space are models built on double the above scale, or 3 inches per ngstrom. At least a few such models can be very useful. Not only are the atoms even easier to see, but one can use electrons and vacancies I inch in diameter, more easily visible through a large room. My own collection includes most of the atomic models of the major group elements, as well as a few molecules and ions.

For smaller group instruction and for special exercises such as those suggested for student laboratory periods in the preceding chapter, as well as for displays and teaching exhibits, a scale one-fifth the first, or 0.3 inch per Angstrom, is very satisfactory. A hydrogen atom is then about one fourth inch in diameter, and carbon, nitrogen, and oxygen atoms about one-half inch in diameter; the largest atoms and ions are about 1.5 inches in diameter.

Materials

From the viewpoint of availability, cost, and ease of construction the foamed polystyrene plastic known as ìstyrofoamî is excellent. Other possible materials are wood, cork, clay, bakelite, asbestos, and paper or cellulose in other forms. No doubt other materials might also be used.

Styrofoam may be purchased in the form of spheres over a range in diameters from 1/2 or 3/4 to 10 inches or more. Intermediate sizes can usually be made by grinding down larger spheres with sandpaper or a power sander, or a power-driven wire brush. The latter is especially effective in reducing the size of large spheres, such as from 10 to 81/2 inches in diameter. Considerable skill is needed to preserve sphericity during such grinding operations. Fortunately, a simpler method is available by which diameters may be reduced by up to 1/2 inch, easily by 1/4 inch, while maintaining a satisfactory degree of sphericity. The ball is rolled in all directions between two smooth, level surfaces, its foamy structure being compressed toward the center by carefully controlled pressure on the rolling surface. If you use a small piece of plate glass for rolling the sphere on a table top, you can see what is happening to the sphere before it becomes uncontrollably misshapen. This rolling process not only decreases the diameter but also compacts and hardens the surface, making it easier to paint and more resistant toward denting and wear in general.

One can place the ball on a smooth table top, and, holding a short, smooth board, or even a hard-covered book, with both hands so that it rests on the ball, cause the ball to roll in all directions by careful manipulation of the board. Frequent inspection of the results is necessary to be sure that deviations from sphericity are caught in time for correction and that the correct diameter is reached. If you have cut down a larger sphere to a smaller one of approximate sphericity, you can accomplish a surprising amount of smoothing of what may initially have been an extremely rough surface.

For making the smaller scale models, 3/4 inch, 1 inch, and 11/4 inches diameters fill most requirements. One can roll a 1-inch diameter ball, for example, down nearly to 1/2-inch diameter, which is approximately the lower limit. For hydrogen atoms on this scale, one must start with spheres not over 1/2-inch diameter (better, smaller), which can be made by sandpapering 3/4-inch diameter balls. Alternatively, they can be made by cutting small cubes of styrofoam, carefully slicing off the corners, and then compressing the foam between thumb and finger to approximate sphericity before rolling to obtain the final smoothing. In fact, you may find it easier to perform the initial compacting of all these smaller spheres between thumb and forefinger, or between the palms, before carrying out the final rolling on a table.

For a guide to size, when making the small-scale models by rolling down larger styrofoam spheres, you will find a circle template invaluable. Such a device is simply a piece of plastic with holes of a large variety of diameters cut in it so it may be used for stencilling. It can be purchased in stationery or drafting supply stores. A series of holes differing each from the next by 1/64 inch in diameter is very satisfactory. Lacking such a device, you can use a good set of drills to bore holes of appropriate diameters in a wooden board or heavy plastic sheetóor even a sharp set of cork borers may do the job. You may wish to make some cardboard guides of similar nature for larger model construction.

Incidentally, I have noticed that rolling 1-inch diameter balls to crush them to smaller diameter builds up a very considerable static charge when done on a plate glass surface. Even on a damp day, this charge is only very slowly lost, much remaining after several hours. Interesting demonstrations of electrostatic fields can be made by dropping such charged balls one by one on to the center of a surface of quiet water, as in a basin. The balls repel one another and move to more symmetrical arrangements.

Styrofoam spheres are easily cut with a knife (better with a serrated or saw like blade), as is necessary when closer than tangential contact between two spheres is desired.

The chief disadvantage of styrofoam though it is not too serious a disadvantage, is its mechanical weakness. It does not break easily but dents too easily. A sphere large enough to have appreciable weight-2 inches in diameter or largeró is likely to acquire a flat area if dropped on the floor, and can be dented by pressing between thumb and finger. Compacting by rolling to decrease the diameter helps strengthen the surface, and even without compacting, the spheres will stand ordinarily careful handling indefinitely long. There is little need to treat them roughly. Repairs can be made by gluing an extra piece of styrofoam in the dent and smoothing with pressure or sandpaper, or by filling with asbestos cement. Large models are heavy enough to place too much strain on the individual joints and they may break at the joint if the model is roughly treated, but again rough treatment can normally be avoided. It has been suggested that the weight of the larger spheres, in the range 6 to 12 inches in diameter, can be reduced if desired by carefully sawing a sphere in half, carving out most of the inside as one might hollow out a pumpkin, and gluing the two hollowed halves back together again.

Styrofoam has become a widely used material for Christmas decorations, and many small local manufacturers of such decorations can supply the spheres. In the holiday season you will find a few sizes on sale at local department stores and other places; you will possibly not wish to pay the retail prices if you need very many of the spheres, but you can probably persuade the store manager to tell you the name of his supplier, who will usually sell by the dozen or the gross at much lower rates. You can also cut your own crudely from chunks of styrofoam plank, such as used by florists or in packing, and these can be rolled quite smooth with a little practice.

Various other materials can be used for inexpensive spheres. Some can be purchased already in ball form, including certain sizes of wood, cork, and bakelite or other plastic such as lucite. Others can easily be made into spheres. Art supply stores often have special powdered modelling clay that can be mixed with water, molded or shaped, and then baked to a fair strength and water resistance. Such clay can be used for small scale models, the shaping being done by rolling a little of the moistened clay between the palms. Ordinary asbestos cement (powdered asbestos), obtainable from paint or hardware stores or plumbing supply houses, can similarly be mixed with water and rolled easily into small spheres. When these have dried in the air, they can then be soaked in sodium silicate solution (commercial ìwater glass,î diluted with one or two volumes of water) for several hours. Your druggist will probably be able to supply you. (If you mix the asbestos with sodium silicate solution in the first place, instead of with water, you will find it difficult to roll smooth balls from it.) When allowed to dry in the air, spheres so treated have much greater strength than the plain asbestos and are satisfactory for model building.

A disadvantage of materials such as clay, asbestos, and plastic (of the unfoamed variety) lies in the difficulty of making permanent connections at the correct bond angles, and with the spheres cut for the proper bond lengths.

Painting

Pigment. A cheap and satisfactory pigment for producing the desired colours is dry tempera. Recommended for the colour scales are the following: black, red, orange, yellow, green, and blue. White may also prove useful. You need not be much of an artist to know that red and yellow mix to give orange, and yellow and blue give green. However, I recommend purchasing orange and green, because our experience was that pleasing oranges and greens did not result from the primary red, yellow, and blue we were able to obtain. Be sure that these purchased colours all look bright and clean. You will then be able to mix very satisfactory intermediate hues, using red and orange for red-oranges, orange and yellow for yellow-oranges, yellow and green for yellow-greens, and green and blue for blue-greens.

We have found not only that different brands of tempera differ in hue of the same colour name, but also that a colour of the same brand is not always constant from container to container. Your problem is to prepare five different red-oranges that are clearly distinguishable from red, from orange, and from one another. Similarly, you will need five different yellow-oranges, five different yellow-greens, and five different blue-greens. With your five basic colours you will have 25 hues. You will want these to be as evenly spaced as possible, but this will happen automatically if you make each as distinct from its neighbours as possible. Be sure to measure and record the relative volumes of pigments in each mixture so that you can reproduce the hue when the supply runs low.

Dry tempera can be mixed very easily merely by shaking in a closed container. About 2-4 ounces of each hue will suffice for a large number of models unless the scale is very large. An initial purchase of 1 pound each of black, red, and blue, and 2 pounds each of green, yellow, and orange should keep you supplied for some time, and at a cost, at time of writing, under one dollar per pound for the pigment.

Colour-Blindness. If you have difficulty distinguishing colours or are worried about the fact that a small percentage of your students are likely to be so handicapped, you may wish a different colour scale. Blues and grays are said to offer less difficulty than any other colors. You may then decide to adopt a black-white-blue scheme. For electronegativity, the range from very low to very high would be from blue through lighter blues, white, and increasingly darker grays to black. The same range would represent partial charge from high positive (blue) through neutral (white) to high negative (black).

Vehicle. Most commercial paints contain solvents that at least soften polystyrene and often dissolve it. Initially, paint for these models was made by mixing tempera with water. This presented the difficulty that water does not wet polystyrene well. A small amount of household dishwashing detergent solved this problem, although brushing rather than dipping was essential because of the rough surface, with crevices still not readily wetted. Increasing the concentration of sizing (glue) in the tempera might have helped improve the adherence of the paint, but as it was, the paint served satisfactorily but not really well. It tended to rub off slightly, and easily came off under abrasive conditions. However, when the models were separately wrapped in tissue and packed together in a trunk, they endured the handling of the nationís railways for thousands of miles without damage either to paint or model.

The Reverend Maurice Blackburn, of Edmonton, Alberta, reported that shellac made a good protective coating, which was superior to the plastic spray I had been using very lightly and recommending (with caution, because the spray is an excellent solvent for polystyrene). This suggested that white shellac might be a satisfactory medium instead of water in the first place. Indeed it is. It wets better, dries faster, gives brighter colors and a surface more resistant to abrasion. The tempera cuts the natural gloss of the shellac, giving a clean, velvety appearance that is very appealing. The durability of the color cannot yet be vouched for, but at least no change is noticeable after several months.

Where dipping is convenient, it appears to be as satisfactory as brushing, especially when shellac is the medium, or vehicle. This is notably true when the spheres have been rolled and thus have a smoother surface. It is a very effective and rapid method especially for the small-scale models. You merely drop the ball into a jar of paint and when you have fished it out, it is painted. This is a real timesaver in eliminating the need of cleaning brushes. The freshly painted sphere can be placed to dry on a piece of newspaper, avoiding the headlines which tend to come off on the model slightly. If the sphere is then rolled to a fresh position after it has dried for about 10 to 15 minutes, it will not become seriously stuck to the paper in completing the drying, which will take from 15 minutes to an hour longer.

Connectors and Glue

Any glue that does not dissolve styrofoam should be all right. The preparations of brand names ìDuratiteî and ìElmerís Glueallî are among those that are satisfactory. Glue alone can serve to connect styrofoam spheres, and in some more complex models where it is nearly impossible to put connectors in place, glue is the only means of holding the model together. Where possible, however, connectors are strongly recommended, to be used with the glue. These have both temporary and permanent value. Temporarily, until the glue can harden, they can serve to hold atoms together at the correct locations and angles especially when single bond covalence is indicated by tangential contact of the spheres. The permanent value of connectors is derived from the strength they supply. The glue may be unbreakably strong but the styrofoam is not.

A glued spot holding two styrofoam spheres together can easily break out a chunk of foam from one of the spheres. For large models, the larger the connector the better, for the more area the firmer the glued contact. My personal preference is for diamond-shaped wooden connectors about 1/16 inch thick, 1/2 inch at the greatest width, and I to 4 inches long depending on diameters of spheres to be connected. These can be cut from strips of hardwood by making a series of parallel angular cuts.

When two spheres are pushed together from opposite ends of a connector, it may not penetrate the two spheres evenly, but, encountering a tougher region in one sphere, may penetrate the other almost exclusively. This is the chief reason for the diamond shapeóthe resistance to penetration increases with depth, and an even placement of the connector is ordinarily assured.

Styrofoam is easily penetrated. You can hold between thumb and forefinger a connector such as described above and thrust it into a sphere readily without making a preliminary slot or hole. A simple procedure is to place a generous drop of glue on the sphere at the bond location and thrust the connector straight through the middle of the glue into the sphere until it reaches the widest part of the diamond. Then spread the glue generously over the protruding surface of the connector and thrust the connector into the second atom.

For the small scale models pipe cleaners work very well as connectors. Cut the pipe cleaner into appropriate lengths, using a wire cutter. At the point to be connected, thrust a sharp pencil point into the sphere about 1/4 inch. Place a drop of glue over the hole and thrust the connector in, to the desired depth. Repeat, preparing the other atom for connection and then push the atoms together until they make satisfactory contact and the pipe cleaner section is completely concealed. When the glue is partly but not entirely dry, the bond angles can be given final adjustment if necessary.

Electrons and Vacancies

The choice of materials to be used to represent the electrons and vacancies of the outer shell, both in the atomic models and in the molecular models where desired, depends on the scale of the models. For the large scale, 1-inch diameter styrofoam spheres fastened to the atomic surface like other atoms by glue and connector are satisfactory. For the medium scale, the electron and vacancy balls cannot be more than about 1/4 to 3/4 inch in diameter. Plastic balls of this size range are very inexpensive (e.g., bakelite or lucite). If not purchased in the needed color they may be painted and glued to the atoms in the desired locations.

Wooden or plastic beads can similarly be painted and fastened to the atomic sphere by a combination of glue and nail. From the viewpoint of strength this is better as small balls merely glued are easily broken loose from the styrofoam simply by a tearing of the styrofoam. For the small-scale models, white and black glass-headed pins, which are cut the right length with wire cutters, are ideal. If these cannot be obtained, one can purchase in a hobby shop, black and white beads about 1/16 to 1/8 inch in diameter, such as are used in ìbeadcraftî making beaded belts and other designs on leather goods. These are very inexpensive. Short common pins, about 1/2 inch long, and glue are suitable for fastening these beads to the atoms. For either the glass-headed pin or the bead-and-pin, one first places a small spot of glue on the atomic surface, then thrusts the pin into the atom at that point. When common pins and beads are used, the pinheads can easily be touched up later with white or black paint-tempera plus shellac.

Locating Bond Positions

You may wish to improvise some type of jig for locating the positions on the atomic spheres for attaching other atoms at the proper bond angles. However, a good eye for symmetry and a few simpler aids can make such a jig unnecessary, especially with styrofoam which lends itself well to minor corrections. The most common angles to locate are those of a regular tetrahedron, 109 28'. If you have a number of spheres of the same size, you may wish to prepare a simple guide for locating these positions. Such a guide is based on the fact that the diameter of a circle which would circumscribe any three corners of a tetrahedron is 0.93 times the diameter of the sphere which exactly encloses the entire tetrahedron. Draw on a piece of stiff cardboard or plastic sheet a circle 0.93 times the diameter of the spheres you intend to use as tetrahedral atoms. Inscribe an equilateral triangle in this circle and mark the points where its corners touch the circle. Cut out the circle, leaving a hole with the three points marked on its edge. Now, if you hold a sphere firmly in this hole, with a sharp pencil you can make on it the three points. These are three of the four corners of the inscribed tetrahedron. The fourth corner can be located visually as equidistant from the other three.

Ordinarily, a simple drawing on paper, consisting of a series of concentric circles of the approximate sizes of the atomic spheres you will use, with straight lines from its center indicating a variety of common angles, such as 90 , 100 , 109 28', 120 , etc., can serve as a guide for most purposes. Simply hold the sphere over such a drawing so that it is properly centered to fit the appropriate circle, and mark the positions on its surface. When, for example, you have thus marked two positions making a bond angle of 109 28' (toothpicks serving well as markers), you may find the other two corners of the terathedron in either of the following ways. You can select visually a point that makes an equilateral triangle with the first two, on one side of them, and then select another point that makes an equilateral triangle with the first two, on the other side of them. Alternatively, you can locate a point midway between the first two points and then another point exactly opposite this one on the other side of the sphere. Then locate two points equidistant from this last point, at the same distance as the first two points are distant from the point midway between them. These two new points form a straight line that is perpendicular to the line formed by the original two points. With a little practice you can thus assemble molecular tetrahedra visually, and the final test will be the symmetry of the completed structure. Even after the glue has dried, you can make minor alterations in bond angles by pressing the two ìatomsî firmly together and applying a little extra pressure in the direction needed. New glue can then be added around this joint to tighten it again.

Construction Patterns

For all models which include multiple bonding, which means closer than tangential approach of bonded atoms, you will find it helpful to prepare a simple two-dimensional pattern. All you need is paper, compass, ruler, and protractor. First make a skeleton of the model, or portion of the model, consisting of straight lines forming the correct bond angles. The nucleus of one atom will be at the intersection of two or more such lines. Measure, to the correct scale, the exact inter nuclear distance to the-next atom and mark a point there to represent its nucleus. Then, using these nuclei as centers, draw a circle of the correct radius for the atom in the compound, around each. Where these circles overlap, as they will if multiple bonding is involved, the correct line at which to cut off each sphere is indicated. Simply hold the sphere on a table resting directly over the circle that represents it, and cut off the segment as indicated. Be careful to make your cut straight down. Before attaching the spheres together, you can smooth out the two cut surfaces by pressing the two surfaces gently together and scrubbing them over one another. Such construction patterns are not only needed for help with multiple bonds, but they are also useful as guides in fastening the spheres at the correct bond angles.

Building Models

Complete details for building many atomic, molecular, and crystal models are given in the final section of this chapter. You certainly need not be limited to the models listed therein, for you can easily calculate all you need to know for the construction of many others, especially with the help of the tables provided. The following procedure is typical:

1. From the chemical formula and the electronegativities of the component elements, calculate the electronegativity of the combination.

2. From the electronegativity of the combination, calculate the covalent radius of each atom in combination. This task should be greatly aided by the data from which all you need to do is interpolate if the radii you want are not already in the table. From these radii, and the appropriate factor for whatever scale you have chosen, you can determine what diameters are needed for each atomic sphere.

3. From the electronegativity of the combination, calculate the partial charge on each combined atom.

4. Look up the structural data from some compilation of experimentally determined structures. You will find the book, *Interatomic Distances*, edited by L.E. Sutton and published by The Chemical Society, London, very useful. *Structural Inorganic Chemistry*, Second Ed., A. F. Wells, Oxford University Press, is an excellent reference.

In such a source you should find bond lengths and bond angles. Certain of the bond lengths or angles may not be given, or, you may not find any information about the compound of which you would like to build a model. You may not even have access to any of the sources named above. This need not discourage your making a molecular model if you are reasonably sure from your general chemical knowledge which atoms are attached to which. You can then reason that the single bond lengths are not likely to differ substantially from the sum of the calculated radii. This table also suggests factors for determining the multiple bond lengths from the single bond lengths, which are the sums of the calculated atomic radii.

5. Obtain the desired number and size of spheres, reducing larger spheres if necessary to exact dimensions. Also obtain the necessary number and size of connectors. Paint the spheres and let dry.

6. Draw full-scale patterns to guide your cutting segments from the spheres if necessary to make the bond length correct. Remember that no one knows for certain

how far one atom extends, and where the other begins, along the line of a bond. What is known definitely, and often with much greater accuracy than will be significant in your models, is the distance between the two nuclei. If this distance is correct and the bond angles are correct in your model, the model shows all that is definitely known from experiment, whatever may be the relative sizes of the component atoms.

In most molecules you will find the reported bond length to be equal to or less than the sum of the calculated single covalent bond radii. However, occasionally, and especially in ìionicî crystals, you will find the inter nuclear distance to be greater than this. This means that the individual spheres chosen as the atoms will not come in contact. At least three ways out of this dilemma are possible. (1) Increase the diameter of the more negative atom by the necessary amount to permit contact at the correct inter nuclear distance. The justification for this is that a negatively charged atom is much more easily deformed (polarized) than is a positively charged atom, and in the crystal the negative ion is ordinarily completely surrounded by positive ions which exert a highly polarizing influence and might logically be thought of as causing expansion of the electron sphere of the negative atom. (2) If justified by the type of compound, use ionic instead of calculated covalent radii. This is the most conventional, although not necessarily the most accurate, method. These are ìGoldschmidtî radii-empirical radii assigned from observations of many crystalline compounds. Such radii have the merit that their sums do usually give correct or nearly correct internuclear distances in many crystalline compounds. (3) Use the atomic spheres in sizes calculated for covalent radii-in-combination, but use extended connectors so that the spheres are connected with the correct internuclear distance, even though the spheres themselves are not in contact in the model.

7. Cut each sphere as necessary for connecting.

8. Using glue and connectors, assemble the model. If the model is intricate, you may wish to assemble only part

at a time, waiting for the glue to harden before proceeding to the next part. A disadvantage of this is that small irregularities in size and angle have a disgusting habit of multiplying instead of cancelling one another. In fact, this seems to be one of the chief laws of model construction: Errors never cancel, always add or multiply.

You will probably discover the inexorable validity of this law the first time you try to assemble an intricate crystal model, or even a benzene ring. If you can discover, while all joints are still wet, that certain atoms fail to meet where they should, or the model is lopsided, or the spaces that ought to be identical are actually quite different, you can sometimes make corrections more easily. On the other hand, some corrections cannot readily be made until a certain amount of rigidity is present, or you will introduce new and worse errors while correcting the old.

If major reorientation becomes necessary, you need not abandon the model, for holes left by changing the position of joints can easily be plugged. For example, you can cut a scrap of styrofoam itself approximately to fit the hole, wet it with glue, shove it in place by brute force, and after smoothing the exterior, repaint the surface. Should this result in paint smears on adjacent atoms, simply use a knife to scrape them off when dry and repaint. No one will ever guess that your original effort was so miserable.

Specific Instructions

Atomic Models

The procedure is straightforward. Obtain or cut spheres to the correct size, paint the appropriate color, let dry, and fasten the electrons and vacancies at the correct positions on the surface.

Molecular Models: General

The construction of these is described under the categories: ìelements,î ìbinary compounds,î ìternary compounds,î and ìfour elements or more.î For reference the compounds are numbered consecutively.

Models of the Elements

For most of the metallic elements, the usual states of aggregation can be represented by one or two of only three principal crystalline forms. Construction of these forms, (1) body-centered cubic, (2) face-centered cubic, and (3) hexagonal

Hydrogen: Fasten two atoms together in tangential contact.

Helium: Just one atom suffices. Such a model may seem superfluous, but actually it serves to emphasize the extremely important fact that inert atoms do not form bonds, even with one another.

Boron: In at least one crystalline form of the element, as well as in certain borides, boron atoms occur in icosahedral (20-faced) clusters of 12 atoms each. One of these clusters can be represented by fastening 12 spheres together as follows: First, make a triangle, each sphere joined to the other two. Then make three more such triangles, and group the four triangles together in as spherical a form as possible, and attach them.

Carbon: Diamond: The model contains 23 atoms. Assemble in tangential contact so that each interior carbon is connected to four other carbons at the corners of a regular tetrahedron surrounding it. When you have one layer of such interconnected tetrahedra resting on the table top, you may observe that two alternatives are possible for building the next layer. One would result in the wurtzite structure, the other in the diamond or sphalerite (zincblende) structure. Be sure you proceed correctly for the diamond structure, as the other form is not known in carbon.

Graphite: The bond length in graphite is 1.42 . The bond angles in the planar layers are all 120 . The inter-layer distance is 3.35 . Draw, as a pattern, a circle the size selected for a carbon atom, and at the correct inter center distance to represent 1.42 , draw a second circle. These circles will intersect at a line indicating where the spheres must be cut. Draw two more circles, thus forming an equilateral triangle around the central circle (bond angles 120), and the pattern is complete. Hold each atomic sphere over the pattern and cut off the three segments. This will test your skill in cutting and your patience a little later when you begin to connect the atoms into hexagonal rings. Be sure the condensed rings are planar within a layer. Finally, the layers may be held at the proper separation by pieces of wood, which will be made relatively inconspicuous later by painting black or with camouflage paint.

One layer goes over another so that a carbon of one layer is centered over each hole in the other layer. You will observe two alternatives in the placement of a third layer. These lead to two different modifications of graphite. In the pictured model layer one exactly corresponds to layer three.

Nitrogen: The bond length is 1.10 . Draw the pattern to scale and cut two spheres where needed, and join them together.

Oxygen: Same as nitrogen, except that the bond length is 1.21 .

Halogens: Connect two atoms in tangential contact.

Silicon: Like diamond.

Phosphorus: Connect three atoms in tangential contact to form a triangle, and place the fourth atom on the center of the triangle so it is connected to each of the other three. Alternatively, make two pairs of atoms and then join them together into the tetrahedron.

Sulfur: Bond angles are 105 . Attach in tangential contact two sulfur atoms to one, making an angle of 105 . Prepare another group of three just like the first. Hold the two trios so that their terminal atoms form a planar square, and attach them together by two more atoms so that the two new atoms form another planar square with the central atoms of the first two trios. This square will be parallel to the first square and oriented with its corners nears the middle of each side of the first square.

Binary Compounds

Most of the data for construction are tabulated. The tables, in order, are, 10-6 Binary Oxygen Compounds, 10-8 Binary Hydrogen Compounds, 10-9 Binary Fluorine Compounds, 10-10 Binary Chlorine Compounds, 10-11 Binary Bromine Compounds, 10-12 Binary Iodine Compounds, and 10-13 Binary Sulfur Compounds. Within these tables the order is that of major groups of the periodic table, then subgroups, then any miscellaneous related compounds. For each compound, the following information is given: reference number, formula, electronegativity, radii of the two atoms in , the diameter in inches for each atom on each of the three suggested scales, 100 times the partial charge, the colors, the type, and, where needed, the bond angle. The type is indicated by letter, for which the following instructions apply:

A. These are compounds containing only one single bond per gas molecule. The spheres should be attached in only slightly more than tangential contact.

B. These are molecules whose two single bonds are linear. Tangential contact is made at opposite sides of the central sphere.

C. These molecules are planar triangles with the same tangential contact for each bond and 120 angles between the bonds.

D. These are molecules in which the central atom is surrounded tetrahedrally by four pairs of electronsó which may or may not be involved in the bonds. When the bond angle is known to deviate significantly from the 109 28' tetrahedral angle, it is listed in the last column. This only occurs when at least one of the four electron pairs is not used in the bonding. The individual bonds are formed just as in types A, B, and C.

A. These compounds are either giant molecules held together in all directions by covalent bonds, or ìionicî crystals having no individual molecules. For these, crystal models would be useful, but an ìatom-pairî model will at least show the calculated radii and the charges on the two kinds of atoms. The painted spheres, one of each kind of element, are not attached directly but at opposite ends of a connecting rod which holds them a clearly visible distance apart. The purpose of such a model must be carefully explained as limited to representing (1) the condition of the component atoms, and (2) if outer electrons and vacancies are included, as they should be, the number of each and thus the tendency to condense.

B. These are compounds for which special instructions on model construction would be helpful. Usually these models require drawing a simple full-scale diagram to be used as a pattern.

Binary Compounds, Specific Instructions

4) H_2O_2. Attach one H to each O. Connect the two Oís together so each OOH angle is about 100 , and, when viewed along the OóO axis, the two OH bonds make an angle of about 90 .

23) CO. Make a pattern, showing where to cut the two spheres so that the bond length corresponds to 1.13 . The two atoms are taken to be of equal radius because apparently the arrangement of electrons to form a triple bond counteracts the expected polarity effect. This also is why

yellow is suggested as the colour; the calculated colors would be 5P for C and 5N for O. Connect the two spheres through the cut areas.

24) CO_2. This molecule is linear, with bond length 1.15 and carbon in the middle. Draw a pattern on paper and cut segments from the carbon and oxygen spheres to give the proper bond length. Assemble.

25) CO_3 =. This ion is planar, with bond lengths 1.31 , and 120 angles. A pattern is needed. Cut the atoms as required and assemble, attaching the three oxygen to the central carbon.

32) N_2O. Linear, NNO, with NóN 1.13 and NóO 1.19 . Draw a pattern and cut off segments of spheres to give the proper bond length, and connect.

33) NO. Bond length 1.15 . Draw a pattern and cut spheres for the correct bond length, and connect.

34) N_2O_3. Assume ONONO structure, which is speculative but reasonable. Bond lengths are 1.13 for the terminal oxygen to nitrogen, and 1.17 for the middle oxygen to nitrogen. NON angle is 105 , and ONO angle is 120 . Assume a planar structure and construct a pattern for cutting the atoms and connecting.

35) NO_2. The two oxygen are attached to the nitrogen at an angle of 132 and a distance of 1.19 . Draw a pattern, cut off segments, and attach.

36) N_2O_5. Assemble a NO_3 group similar to that of HNO_3. Assemble an NO2 group similar to the italicized part of the O_2 *NOH*, and then attach its nitrogen to the singly bonded oxygen of the first group so that the NON angle is about 105 , and with the two NO $_2$ groups at right angles to one another.

37) NO_3 - Draw a pattern with three oxygen forming an equilateral triangle around nitrogen, with 120 bond angles and bond lengths about 1.24 . Cut spheres and attach.

38) P_4O_6. This molecule can be considered to be derived from a tetrahedron of phosphorus atoms, only instead of their being in direct contact, they are held together by oxygen bridges. To one atom of phosphorus, attach three oxygen making 99 angles. Next, attach a phosphorus atom to each of these oxygen so that the POP angle is 128 *and* this P atom is directed toward the midpoint between the other two oxygen. Finally, attach the remaining three oxygen as bridges of these last three phosphorus atoms. All six oxygen bridges should be symmetrically directed *away* from the edge of the P_4 tetrahedron.

39) P_4O_{10}. Assemble a P_4O_6 group like No. 38. Then cut a segment off each P atom at opposite side from the tetrahedron and from each of the four new oxygens so that they can be connected, one oxygen to each phosphorus, at the corners of the tetrahedron and at bond lengths of 1.39 .

40) PO_4 =. The oxygens and phosphorus must be cut to permit attachment of four oxygens to phosphorus at corners of a regular tetrahedron with bond lengths of 1.54 .

41) As_4O_6. This molecule resembles No. 38. The bond angles are OAsO 100 and AsOAs 128 .

43) Sb_4O_6. Like 38 and 41.

47) SO_2. Cut off segments of sulfur and two oxygens to represent bond lengths of 1.43 , with OSO bond angle of 120 , and connect.

48) SO_3. Like SO_2, 47, except complete the triangle of oxygen atoms in a plane surrounding the sulfur. Same bond length and angles.

49) SeO_2. In this compound are continuous OóSeóO-chains with another oxygen joined to each selenium at a slightly shorter distance. SeOSe angles are 125 and OSeO angles 90 . The O (bridge) SeO (nonbridge) angle is 98 . Some of the nonbridging oxygens are hidden from view in the photo. The selenium atoms of a chain are all in the same

plane, and in a plane parallel to this are all the nonbridging oxygen atoms.

53) SO_4 =. In this ion, the oxygens surround the sulfur in a regular tetrahedral manner, with bond lengths of 1.44 , which requires drawing a pattern and cutting the spheres accordingly.

55) ClO_2. This is a bent molecule, with angle 116 and bond length 149 . Draw a pattern and cut the atoms, and connect, chlorine in the center.

56) Cl_2O_7. Structure not known. Suggest $(ClO_3)_2O$, as shown in photo. Cut off three segments from each chlorine, at corners of a tetrahedron, and one from each of six oxygens to prepare for multiple bond connections. Connect three oxygens to each chlorine, flat to flat area. Then attach the seventh oxygen to the fourth tetrahedral corner of each chlorine, making the bond angle about 110 .

57) ClO_4^-. Four oxygen atoms are double-bonded to the chlorine at the corners of a regular tetrahedron. Cut off the atoms as required and assemble.

74) B_2H_6. First attach two hydrogens to each boron at an angle of 120 . Then join the two BH_2 groups by two hydrogens as follows. Use two hydrogens about 20 per cent larger than the other four, in order for the boron-boron distance to be correct. Place the two BH_2 groups B to B so the hydrogens are as far apart as possible, and the groups, parallel to the table top, are all in the same plane. Have the borons separated by sufficient space that the BóB length corresponds to 1.77 . Attach one bridging hydrogen on top between the two borons, and the other just opposite it, so that the plane of the bridging hydrogens and the borons is perpendicular to the plane of the original two BH_2 groups.

75) B_4H_{10}. Attach two borons barely in tangential contact. Attach a third boron to each of these two by means of two bridging hydrogens, the three borons and two hydrogens being in the same plane. The third boron should be 1.85 from each of the first two. Then attach a fourth boron similarly to

form a second hydrogen-bridged triangle like the first, with the first two borons forming a common side. The angle between the two triangles is 118 . Finally, attach two hydrogens to each apical boron and one to each base boron, making the molecule as symmetrical as possible. This means that the two terminal hydrogens on each boron come as close as possible to forming a regular tetrahedron with the two bridging hydrogens, and the single hydrogen on each of the central boron pair is as far from all the other bonds to that boron as possible.

76) B_5H_9. Attach two borons tangentially. Then attach three other borons to one of the first two so that they are about 0.3" apart (medium scale) and form the base of a square pyramid on top of which rests the fifth boron. Take four bridging hydrogens, each 20 per cent larger than the regular size hydrogens, and bridge the four 0.3 inch gaps at a position directly opposite the apical boron. Now connect the five regular size hydrogens, one to each boron, as far from all other bonds as possible.

77) $B_{10}H_{14}$. Connect two borons tangentially. On each side of this pair, at the junction, attach one more boron, so it is connected to each of the pair. The four borons thus assembled are not quite planar, one of the last borons being about 0.5 inch (medium scale) out of the plane of the triangle formed by the other three. Now, to each of these last two borons, attach one boron so that it forms an angle of about 100 with the near plane of the first four. The idea is to construct a basketlike model. The last pair of borons will be separated from one another by a distance about 0.5 inch greater than the separation of the second pair of borons to be added. Now attach four more borons, two to each of the last connected borons, so that each also attaches to one of the initial pair of borons and nearly attaches to one of the second pair of borons. You will thus have formed a basket. The last borons added leave about 0.5 inch gap at each side of the basket rim. The basket bottom closely resembles the B_{12} cluster of elementary boron.

Now you will need four bridging hydrogens each about 20 per cent larger than the ten other hydrogens. Attach these four at the top rim of the basket, so that they connect all but the two 0.5 inch gaps previously mentioned. Taken alone, these four bridging hydrogens form a square. Now connect one regular size hydrogen to each of the ten borons at the point farthest from all other bonds.

81) Ga_2H_6. Like B_2H_6, 74.

86) C_2H_6. Mark four tetrahedral positions on each carbon. Attach three hydrogens to each carbon, and then the two methyl groups together. The most stable configuration would be the ìstaggeredî position for the hydrogens, looking along the carbon-carbon axis, so all six hydrogens are uniformly distributed in the field of vision.

86a) C_2H_2 (or C_6H_6). Acetylene: Cut segments from the two carbons so their bond length will represent 1.20 . Connect them, and at opposite sides attach one hydrogen to each carbon, making the whole molecule linear.

Benzene: Cut segments from the carbons to permit 1.39 bond lengths and 120 angles. Connect the carbon atoms in threes, and then attach the two trios together, forming the planar ring of six. Finally, attach one hydrogen to each carbon in the same plane as the ring, evenly spaced so the HCC angles are 120 .

86b) C_2H_4. Cut two carbon atoms so their bond length will be 1.34 . Connect them. Attach two hydrogens to each carbon so all atoms are in the same plane and all bond angles are 120 .

87) See benzene, 86a.

88) C_7H_{16}. n-Heptane: Attach all seven carbons in ìstraightî (zigzag) chain, with 109 bond angles. Completely fill the remaining tetrahedral positions with hydrogen atoms. ìTriptane,î 2,2,3-trimethylbutane: Attach four carbons in a ìstraightî chain (109 angles). Prepare three CH_3 groups and attach two to carbon (2) and one to carbon (3). Completely fill the remaining tetrahedral positions with hydrogens.

89) $C_8 H_{18}$. ìIsooctane,î 2,2,4-trimethylpentane: Connect five carbons in ìstraightî chain. Prepare three methyl groups, and attach two of them to carbon (2) and one to carbon (4). Fill the remaining tetrahedral positions with hydrogens.

98) $N_2 H_4$. Attach two hydrogens to each nitrogen at an angle of 109 . Attach the nitrogen together making the same angle with NH bonds, but the molecule is not symmetrical. The exact orientation is unknown, but probably resembles that of $H_2 O_2$ (4).

100) $P_2 H_4$. Probably like hydrazine, 98.

129) $B_2 F_4$. Attach two fluorines to each boron at 120 . Then connect the two boron atoms so the two BF_2 planes are mutually perpendicular.

136) $C_2 F_6$. Like $C_2 H_6$ (86).

139) $Si_2 F_6$. Similar.

146) $N_2 F_4$. Probably resembles hydrazine (98).

148) PF_5. Attach three fluorines to phosphorus in the same plane, forming an equilateral triangle with the phosphorus at the center. Directly above this plane attach a fourth fluorine to the phosphorus. On the opposite side of the phosphorus, attach the fifth fluorine. Thus formed: a trigonal bipyramid.

153) SF_4. Possibly like PF_5 above with the fifth fluorine missing.

154) SF_6. Attach four fluorines to the sulfur in tangential contact, forming a planar square with sulfur at the center. Then attach a fifth fluorine directly over the sulfur perpendicular to the square, and a sixth fluorine exactly opposite this fifth. Result: six equally placed fluorines forming a regular octahedron around the sulfur.

155) $S_2 F_{10}$. Attach five fluorines to each sulfur exactly as in SF_6 (154). Then connect the two sulfurs so that each fills the sixth coordination space of the other, and the fluorine atoms are staggered when viewed along the FSSF

axis (i.e., all 8 equatorial sulfurs are viewed as evenly spaced).

156) SeF_6. Like SF_6, 154.

157) Se_2F_{10}. Like S_2F_{10}.

158) Te_2F_{10}. Like SF_6.

159) Te_2F_{10}. Like 155.

161) ClF_3. Attach one fluorine to chlorine, bond length 1.60 . Then attach each of the remaining two fluorines to the chlorine, at bond length 1.70 , to make bond angles of 87 óall four atoms in the same plane.

162) BrF_3. Probably like 161.

163) BrF_5. Probably tetragonal pyramid with bromine on same side of plane of base as is the fifth fluorine, but closer.

164) IF_5. Probably same.

165) IF_7. Possibly pentagonal bipyramid.

166) B_2C_{14}. Like B_2F_4, 129.

167) B_4Cl_4. Connect the four borons in a tetrahedral cluster. Then attach one chlorine to each boron at the farthest possible distance from the other bonds.

168) Al_2Cl_6. Attach two chlorines to each aluminum, in tangential contact and forming a bond angle of 109 . Then place the two $AlCl_2$ groups on a table with the aluminums near and the chlorines opposite. Arrange so the aluminum surfaces are 1 1/4 inch apart (for the medium scale model). Then bridge them with a chlorine fastened to both, directly above the table. Invert and connect a second bridging chlorine. The bridging chlorines are thus about 1 inch apart and form a plane with the two aluminums that is perpendicular to the plane of the other four chlorine and the aluminums.

169) Ga_2Cl_6. Like 183.

170) In_2Cl_6. Like 183.

171) Si_2Cl_6. Like C_2H_6 (86).

172) PCl_5. Attach three chlorines tangentially to phosphorus, at corners of an equilateral triangle around the phosphorus, with 120 bond angles. Then attach just barely tangentially, the other two chlorines, one directly above the triangle, the other directly below, forming a trigonal bipyramid. The bond lengths for the last two chlorines (apical) are slightly greater than the others (equatorial).

173) S_2 Cl_2. Connect tangentially one chlorine to each sulfur. Then connect the two sulfurs so that the SSCl bond angles are 104 and the plane of the two sulfurs and one chlorine makes an angle of 98 with the plane of the two sulfurs and the second chlorine.

174) Se_2 Cl_2. Like 203.

175) $SeCl_4$. Probably like 207.

176) $TeCl_4$. Like PF_5, but with one equatorial position vacant.

177) ICl_3. Probably like 161.

178) $ZnCl_2$, crystal. Attach six chlorines to one zinc with 90 angles, forming thus a regular octahedron. Do this by first attaching two chlorines, one at each side of a zinc, so the three atoms form a straight line. Then, at right angle to this line, attach two more chlorines at opposite positions on the zinc. You now have a square of chlorine atoms with zinc at the center. Now attach one chlorine directly above the square, another directly below. This is the regular octahedron. Now, allow the octahedron to rest on three of its chlorines. The other three chlorines will be held in the air. The zinc chloride crystal lattice consists of layers-each layer a sandwich, a plane of chlorine atoms on the table, a parallel plane of zinc atoms just above, and a parallel plane of chlorine atoms just above the zinc plane. Build on to the original $ZnCl_6$ group by attaching zinc atoms and other chlorine atoms until you have a layer large enough to suit. A reasonably large section contains about 11 zinc atoms and 22 chlorine atoms.

179) Al_2 Br_6. Like 183.

328) $BrCH_3$ ó C H_3 Br. C 2.3"d, O; H 1"d, 2P; Br 3.6"d. 5N. Attach the three hydrogens and the bromine to the carbon, with tangential contact and all bond angles 109 .

329) BrH_3 SióSiH_3 Br. Si 3"d, 7P; H 1"d, O; Br 3.7"d, 6N. Same as 328.

330) Br_2 CH_2 ó C H_2 Br . C 2.3"d, 2P; H 1"d, 4P; Br 3.6"d, 4N. Attach all other atoms tangentially to the carbon at 109 angles.

331) Br_2 OSóSOBr_2. S 3"d, 4P; O 2.3"d, 4N; Br 3.4"d, O. Cut off S and O atoms to make the bond lengths representative of 1.45A. Connect. Making 109 angles with the SO bond and with each other, attach the two bromines tangentially to the sulfur.

332) Br_3 CHóCHBr_3. C 2.2"d, 3P; H 0.9"d, 5P; Br 3.5"d, 3N. Like 330.

333) Br_3 OPóPOBr_3. P 2.9"d, 7P; O 2.4"d, 5N, Br 3.4"d, 1N. Cut off the oxygen and phosphorus atoms to represent a bond length of 1.41 . Connect. Attach the three bromine atoms tangentially to the phosphorus so that it is surrounded by four atoms tetrahedrally.

334) Br_3 PSóPSBr_3. P 2.9"d, 6P; S 3"d, IP; Br 3.5"d, 3N. Like 333. PóS bond length, 1.89 .

335) $CaCO_3$. Ca ion, 3"d, 12P. C03 ion, see 25.

336) $CClH_3$ ó CH_3Cl. C 2.3 d, O; H 1"d, 3P; C1 3.2"d, 6N. Like 328.

337) CCl_2 F_2. C 2.3"d, 7P; Cl 3"d, O; F 2.5"d, 5N. Surround carbon with the other atoms tetrahedrally.

338) CCl_2 H_2 ó C H_2 Cl_2. C 2.3"d, 3P; H 1"d, 4P; Cl 3.2"d, 5N. Like 330.

339) CCl_3 HóCHCl_3. C 2.3"d, 4P; H 0.8"d, 6P; Cl 3"d, 4N. Like 332.

340) CFH_3 ó C H_3 F. C 2.3"d, 2P; H 1"d, 4P; F 2.5"d, 8N. Like 328.

341) CF_2H_2óCH_2F_2. C 2.2"d, 4P; H 0.8"d, 6P; F 2.4"d, 7N. Like 330.

342) CF_3HóCHF_3. C 2.1"d, 7P; H 0.8"d, 8P; F 2.3"d, 5N. Like 332.

343) CHI_3. C 2.3"d, O; H 1"d, 2P; I 4"d, 1N. Like 332.

344) CHO_3óHCO_3-.

Prepare two cuts on carbon and one on each of two oxygens as in CO_3 = (25). Connect. At the third corner of an equilateral triangle around the carbon, attach the OH tangentially, HOC angle about 105 , and the hydrogen coplanar with the rest of the ion.

345) CHNóHCN. C 2.3""d, 1P; H 1"d, 4P; N 2.4"d, 4N. Cut the carbon and nitrogen atoms to represent a bond length of 1.16 , and connect. Then attach the hydrogen to the carbon exactly opposite the nitrogen, so the molecule is linear.

346) CH_2OóHCHO. C 2.3"d, 2P; H 1"d, 4P; O 2.4"d, 7N. Cut the carbon and oxygen to represent a bond length of 1.21 , and connect. Attach the two hydrogens tangentially to the carbon to make an equilateral triangle of two hydrogens and one oxygen around the carbon, with bond angles 120 .

347) CH_2O_2óHCOOH. C 2.3"d, 4P; O 2.4"d, 6N; H 0.8"d, 5P. Cut segments from the carbon and oxygen for a double bond between them. Attach, and then attach the second oxygen at somewhat closer than tangential contact, to the carbon, making the OCO angle 123 . Attach the hydrogen atoms one to the second oxygen, toward the first oxygen, and one to the carbon and symmetrically opposite the two oxygens.

348) CH_3I. C 2.3"d, 1N; H 1.1"d, 1P; I 4.1"d, 2N. Like 328.

349) CH_4OóCH_3OH. C 2.2"d, O; H 1"d, 3p; O 2.4"d, 7N. Attach the three hydrogens and the oxygen to the corners of a regular tetrahedron around the carbon. Then attach the hydrogen to the oxygen at a bond angle of about 109 . All

tangential contact, except that the oxygen and carbon are in slightly closer contact.

350) CH_4SóCH_3SH. C 2.3"d, 1N; H 1.1"d, 1P; S 3.2"d, 4N. Like 349.

351) CH_5NóCH_3NH_2. C 2.3"d, 1N; H 1"d, 2P; N 2.4"d, 5N. Like NH_3 and CH_4 except, attach the NH_2 to the carbon in place of the fourth hydrogen.

352) CH_5N_3óNH_2CNHNH_2, (guanidine). C 2.3"d, 1P; H 1"d, 3P; N 2.4"d, 4N. Prepare two NH_2 groups like NH_3. Cut a third nitrogen and the carbon to represent bond length of 1.26A. Connect. Attach a hydrogen to the cut nitrogen so that the HNC angle is 109 . Attach both NH_2 groups tangentially to the carbon so that the three nitrogen form a triangle around the carbon, with 120 angles.

353) COS. C 2.2"d, 4P; O 2.3"d, 5N; S 3"d, 2P. Cut carbon, oxygen, and sulfur to represent bond lengths of 1.16 for CóO and 1.56 for CS, and to make a linear molecule. Connect.

354) $C_2F_3O_2$óCF_3COO^-. C 2.3"d, 4P; F 2.5"d, 7N; O 2.5"d, 5N. Cut one carbon and two oxygens to represent bond lengths of 1.24 and 120 bond angle. Attach three fluorine to the second carbon at 109 angles. Then connect this carbon tangentially to the first, in the same plane with, and symmetrically opposite from the two oxygens.

355) C_2F_2Oó$(CF_3)_2O$. C 2.1"d, 8P; F 2.2"d, 4N; O 2.2"d, O. Attach three fluorines to each carbon at tetrahedral corners, and then each carbon, at the fourth corner, to the oxygen so that the COC angle is about 125 . Orient CF_3 groups to give minimum interference.

356) C_2H_3NóCH_3CN. C 2.3"d, O; H 1"d, 2P; N 2.4"d, 5N. Like methane and HCN. Methyl carbon should be attached tangentially to the CN carbon, directly opposite from the nitrogen.

357) $C_2H_3O_2$ óCH_3COO-. C 2.4"d, 3N; H 1"d, 1N; O 2.5"d, 9N. Like 354.

358) $C_2H_4O_2$ óCH_3COOH. C 2.3"d, 2P; H 0.8"d, 4P; O 2.4"d, 7N. Attach a methyl group, a double-bonded oxygen, and an OH group to a carbon atom forming a planar triangle with bond angles 120 .

359) C_2H_6O óCH_3CH_2OH. C 2.3"d, O; H 1"d, 2P; O 2.4"d, 8N. Attach three hydrogens tetrahedrally to one carbon and two hydrogens and an OH group similarly to the other carbon. Then join the two carbons at their fourth tetrahedral corners. HOC angle should be about 105 .

360) $(CH_3)_2O$. Same atoms as 359. Form two methyl groups and then attach them to the oxygen with the COC angle 111 .

Orient the two methyl groups to give minimum interference of hydrogens.

361) C_2H_6S óCH_3CH_2SH. C 2.3"d, 1N; H 1.1"d, 1P; S 3.2"d, 4N. Like 359.

362) $(CH_3)_2S$. Like 360.

363) C_2H_7N ó $C_2H_5NH_2$. C 2.3"d, 1N; H 1.1"d, 1P; N 2.4"d, 5N. Like 359, only NH_2 in place of OH. Angles of bonds to nitrogen, about 107 .

364) C_3F_9Nó$(CF_3)_3N$. C 2.1"d, 8P; N 2.4"d, 4P; F 2.3"d, 4N. Attach three fluorines to each carbon at tetrahedral corners. At the fourth corner of each carbon, attach to nitrogen, so that the CNC angle is 114 .

365) C_3H_9Nó$(CH_3)_3N$. C 2.3"d, 1N; H 1.1"d, 1P; N 2.4"d, 5N. Attach three hydrogens to each carbon at tetrahedral corners, and each methyl group at the fourth corner of carbon to the nitrogen, making CNC angles of 109 .

366) C_5H_5N. C 2.5"d, O; H 1"d, 2P; N 2.5"d, 5N. Attach the five carbons and the nitrogen just like the benzene ring, and similarly attach one hydrogen to each carbon.

367) C_6H_5O-. C 2.4"d, 3N; H 1"d, 1N; O 2.6", 9N. Construct like benzene and attach O in place of one hydrogen, at somewhat greater than tangential contact.

368) C_6H_7N ó $C_6H_5NH_2$. C 2.3"d, 1N; H 1"d, 2P; N 2.4"d, 5N. Like benzene and ammonia, only attach third position on the nitrogen to the carbon lacking hydrogen, keeping the nitrogen in the plane of the ring.

369) $C_9H_8O_4$- aspirin. C 2.5"d, 1P; H 1"d, 3P; O 2.5"d, 7N. Form a benzene ring with six carbons and add hydrogen to each of four adjacent carbons. To one of the remaining two ring carbons, attach an acetyl group, through oxygen. To the other, attach the COOH group (as in formic acid). This should be oriented so the acid hydrogen is nearest an oxygen of the acetyl group.

370) $C_{12}H_{22}O_{11}$- sucrose-cane sugar. C 2.5"d, 2P; H 0.8"d, 4P; O 2.5"d, 7N. This molecule contains two rings, one of four carbon and one oxygen atoms, one of five carbons and one oxygen. The bonds are single. Construct Ring A of four carbons and one oxygen, keeping the bond angles 109 to carbon and about 105 to oxygen. Construct Ring B of 5 carbons and one oxygen, bond angles as before. Ring A will be nearly planar, Ring B not. Join the two rings through an outside oxygen atom, as a bridge, attached to a ring carbon next to ring oxygen, on each ring. Then prepare three CH_2 OH groups separately. Attach one to Ring A at the same ring carbon that is attached to the bridge oxygen. Attach another, to Ring A at the ring carbon which is separated from the above mentioned ring carbon by the ring oxygen. Attach the third CH_2OH group to Ring B on the ring carbon analogous to the last mentioned Ring A carbon. Now prepare five OH groups and, with HOC angle of 105 , attach one to each ring carbon, of both rings, that does not already have a CH_2OH group or a bridge oxygen attached to it. This will be two OHís on Ring A and three on Ring B. Finally, complete the valence of all carbon atoms where necessary, by attaching hydrogen atoms.

371) $C_{14} H_9 Cl_5$ -DDT (poorly named, dicblorodipheny-ltrichloroethane). C 2.5"d, 1P; H 1"d, 3P; Cl 3"d, 6N. In this molecule, two chlorophenyl groups and one trichloromethyl group, and one hydrogen, are attached tetrahedrally to one carbon. Prepare two C_6 rings, like benzene, with a chlorine attached to each, in the same plane, and hydrogen attached to each other carbon except to the carbon opposite the chlorine. Attach three cblorines tetrahedrally to another carbon. Attach hydrogen to still another carbon, and complete its tetrahedron by attaching also the two chlorophenyl groups and theCCl_3 group.

372) $C_{20} H_{30}$ O-vitamin A. C 2.3"d, 1N; H 1.1"d, 1 P; O 2.3"d, 1N. Attach five pairs of carbons separately by double bonds, like C_2H_4. Each carbon of these pairs will now form two more bonds at 120 with double bond and each other. To one pair, attach a chain of four carbons so that they form a 6-membered ring having one double bond. This will be close to planar. Attach the remaining four double bonded pairs so they form a planar zigzag chain of 8 carbons attached to one of the double-bonded carbons of the ring. To the single-bonded ring carbon next to this one, attach two methyl groups. Attach a methyl group to the other double-bonded ring carbon. To the other ring carbons attach hydrogens to fill in the vacancies. Now, to the third chain carbon away from the ring, and to the seventh, attach one methyl group each. To the end carbon of this chain, opposite the ring, attach an OH group. Fill any remaining chain vacancies with hydrogen.

373) $C_{21} H_{28} O_5$ -cortisone. C 2.5"d, O; H 1"d, 2P; O 2.5"d, 8N. Better consult a book of biochemistry giving this structure before trying this one which is not too difficult to construct but quite difficult to describe in words.

374) ClHOóHOCl. H 0.8"d, 6P; O 2.5"d, 4N; Cl 3"d, 3N. Attach both hydrogen and chlorine to the oxygen in tangential contact, making a bond angle of 109 .

375) $ClHO_2$ óHOClO. H 0.8"d, 7P; Cl 3"d, 2N; O 2.5"d, 4N. Cut off segments of chlorine and one oxygen to form a double bond, and connect. Attach a second oxygen in tangential

contact, to the chlorine at 109 angle from the first oxygen. Connect hydrogen to this oxygen at 109 angle with the chlorine bond and nearest to the first oxygen.

376) $ClHO_3$ó$HOClO_2$. H 0.8"d, 8P; Cl 3"d, 1N; O 2.5"d, 3N. Cut off two segments at tetrahedral corners of chlorine, as sufficient for two double bonds to oxygen. Cut off similar segments from the two oxygens. Then to a third tetrahedral corner of the chlorine, attach the third oxygen, in tangential contact. To it, attach hydrogen at 109 and either over one other oxygen or midway between the two other oxygens.

377) $ClHO_4$ó$HOClO_3$. H 0.7"d, 8P; Cl 3"d, O; O 2.5"d, 3N. Cut off three segments from three tetrahedral corners around the chlorine. Cut off corresponding segments from each of three oxygens, and connect. Attach the fourth oxygen to the fourth corner of the chlorine, in tangential contact, and to it, one hydrogen, over one of the other oxygens or midway between two of them.

378) ClH_2NóNH_2Cl. N 2.3"d, 3N; H 1"d, 4P; Cl 3.2"d, 5N. Attach the two hydrogens and the chlorine to the nitrogen, making bond angles of 109 .

379) ClH_3SióSiH_3Cl. Si 3"d, 7P; H 1.2"d, O; Cl 3.3"d, 7N. Like CH_3Cl.

380) Cl_2OSó$SOCl_2$. O 2.3"d, 3N; S 3"d, 5P; Cl 3"d, 1N. Cut the sulfur and oxygen atoms to represent a bond length of 1.45 . Connect, and then attach the two chlorines to the sulfur so that the ClSCl angle is 114 and the OSCl angle is 106 .

381) Cl_2O_2SóSO_2Cl_2. S 3"d, 5P; O 2.3"d, 3N; Cl 3"d, O. Cut the sulfur and oxygen atoms for an SO bond length of 1.43 and an OSO angle of 120 . Then attach the two chlorines to the sulfur so that their plane is perpendicular to the OSO plane and the ClSCl angle is 112 .

382) Cl_3 HSIóSiHCl_3. Si 3"d, 7P; H 1.2"d, O; Cl 3.3"d, 8N. Attach hydrogen and chlorines tetrahedrally to the silicon.

383) Cl_3OPóPOCl_3. P 3"d, 8P; O 2.5"d, 4N; Cl 3"d, 2N. Cut the phosphorus and oxygen atoms for a bond length of 1.45 and connect. Then attach the three chlorines to the phosphorus with ClPCl angle of 104 .

384) Cl_3PSóPSCl_3. P 2.9"d, 7P; S 3.1"d, 3P; Cl 3.1"d, 4N. Like 383, except cut phosphorus and sulfur for a bond length about 1.9 .

385) FH_3 SióSiH_3 F. Si 3"d, 8P; H 1"d, 1P; F 2.5"d, 9N. Attach the hydrogens and fluorine tetrahedrally around the silicon.

386) FNOóNOF. N 2.2"d, 4P; O 2.3"d, 1N; F 2.3"d, 4N. Cut the nitrogen and oxygen atoms for a bond length of 1.13 , and connect. Attach the fluorine to the nitrogen so that the FNO angle is 110 .

387) F_2OSóSOF_2. S 3"d, 6P; O 2.3"d, O; F 2.3"d, 4N. Like $SOCl_2$.

388) F_2 O_2 SóSO_2 F_2. S 3"d, 7P; O 2.3"d, O; F 2.3"d, 4N. Cut the sulfur and oxygens for a bond length of 1.4 , and an OSO angle of 130 , and connect. Attach the two fluorines to the sulfur in a plane perpendicular to the OSO plane, with an FSF angle of 93 .

389) F_3OPóPOF_3. P 2.7"d, 10P; O 2.3"d, 1N; F 2.3"d, 4N. Like 383.

390) F_3PSóPSF_3. P 2.8"d, 9P; S 2.9"d, 5P; F 2.3"d, 5N. Like 384.

391) HNO_3. H 0.8"d, 7P; N 2.2"d, 2P; O 2.3"d, 4N. Cut the nitrogen and two of the oxygens for bond lengths of 1.22 , and 130 bond angle, and connect. Connect the third oxygen so the OóN length represents 1.41 , directly opposite the other oxygens and in the same plane with the NO_2. Attach

hydrogen to the third oxygen in the same plane and with an HON angle of 105 .

392) $H_2 SO_4$. Prepare two OH groups, and attach them and two double-bonded oxygens to four corners of a tetrahedron around the sulfur, cutting the sulfur and double-bonded oxygens in preparation. H 0.8"d, 6P; S 3"d, 3P; O 2.3"d, 4N.

393) $Zn(NH_3)_4$ ++ Zn 3.5"d, 9P; N 2.3"d, 3N; H 0.8"d, 5P. Construct four ammonia molecules and attach them tetrahedrally around the zinc.

Miscellaneous Compounds Containing Four or More Elements

394) CF_3 COOH. C 2.3"d, 6P; F 2.5"d, 5N; O 2.5"d, 3N; H 0.8"d, 8P. Attach three fluorines to a carbon at three corners of a regular tetrahedron. Cut the second carbon as in acetic acid, and continue as described.

395) BF_3 "$O(CH_3)_2$. B 2.2"d, 8P; F 2.4"d, 8N; C 2.3"d, 2P; H 0.8"d, 4P; O 2.4"d, 6N. Attach tangentially three fluorines and an oxygen around the corners of a regular tetrahedron surrounding boron. Attach three hydrogens at the tetrahedral corners around each carbon, and then at the fourth corner of each carbon, attach to the two tetrahedron corners of oxygen (boron is at the third comer).

396) $C_3 H_5 N_3 O_9$ -nitroglycerin. C 2.3"d, 5P; H 0.8"d, 6P; N 2.3"d, O; O 2.3"d, 5N. Prepare three nitrate groups just like HNO_3 without the hydrogen. Attach the three carbons together with two hydrogens on each terminal carbon and one hydrogen on the central carbon. All carbon bond angles should be 109 . Then to the fourth position of each carbon, attach the single-bonded oxygen of the nitrate group.

397) $C_6 H_8 O_2 N_2$ S-sulfanilamide. C 2.5"d, 1P; H 1"d, 3P; O 2.5"d, 7N; N 2.5"d, 4N; S 3"d, 2N. Make a benzene ring, and at 120 angles attach nitrogen to one carbon, sulfur to

the opposite carbon, and hydrogen to each of the other four carbons in the ring. Add two hydrogens at 109 to the nitrogen, a similar NH $_2$ group to the sulfur, and two oxygens also to the sulfur so it is tetrahedrally surrounded, with the oxygens double-bonded.

398) $C_7H_5N_3O_6$ -TNT-trinitrotoluene. C 2.5"d, 3P; H 0.8"d, 5P; N 2.3"d, 2N; O 2.5"d, 6N. Prepare a benzene ring with one methyl group attached to one carbon. Prepare three NO_2 multiple-bonded groups and attach to the carbons on each side of the methyl and opposite it, so that they are in the plane with the carbon ring. To each of the other two ring carbons, add one hydrogen.

Rock Salt (NACI) Structure

Herein each atom has a coordination number of 6, all neighbors being of opposite kind. To make the model shown in the photo, make three separate checkerboard pattern layers of nine atoms each, two squares with black comers and one with white. Then assemble the layers with the white cornered layer in the middle, forming a black cornered cube.

Cesium Chloride Structure

Each kind of atom is at the center of a cube of 8 atoms of the other kind 8:8 coordination. The structure thus resembles a fluorite structure but with no holes. Enclose one black by 8 whites at the corners of a cube. The bond angle is 70 32' between nearest bond pairs. Then complete a black cube surrounding one of the corner atoms of the white cube. Extend this procedure as far as you like. The pictured model contains 12 atoms of each kind.

Nickel Arsenide: NiAs

Each nonmetal atom is at the center of a triangular prism of six metal atoms of the other kind, instead of the usual octahedron, in 6:6 coordination. Each metal atom is surrounded by a distorted octahedron of nonmetal atoms. The pictured model contains 21 whites and 12 blacks. First, there is a layer of 7 whites, a separated hexagon with one at the center. Next layer is a triangle of 6 blacks. Next is a layer of whites just like the first. Next is a triangle of 6 blacks just like the second only inverted. Next is another hexagonal layer of whites.

First construct a triangular prism of six whites around a black, so that all closest neighbour whites are equally spaced. The spacing is about 0.5 radius between white sphere surfaces. Then construct a second prism with one edge in common with the first, so that six whites are in the same rectangular plane. Using the reverse side of this plane as a base, construct two more such prisms opposite to the first two. You now have the first three layers mentioned above, save for a few blacks. Now build four new prisms above the first four, using their tops for a common base. However, stagger the centers, so they are not one directly above another.

Finally, add three blacks to each black layer, to make triangle points protruding from the hexagonal prism model.

Zinc Blende (Sphalerite) and Wurtzite Structures

These are very similar, except in the positions, relatively, of the layers of tetrahedra. The coordination is 4:4, each atom being surrounded tetrahedrally by four of the other kind.

Corundum Structure: M_2X_3

It is actually identical with the simple cubic lattice of NaCl, except that every third cation location is vacant. This changes the appearance remarkably, especially from certain angles. The model pictured contains four parallel planes that run diagonally through an ordinary cubic structure. These are alternately of black and of white atoms. The total is 32 blacks and 16 whites.

One of many possible ways to construct such a model is to begin by forming a square of blacks around a white. Using one edge of this square as a common edge of an adjacent square in the same plane, attach another white to this edge and complete the square. You now should have 8 balls in a rectangular plane two black squares with a side in common using 6 blacks, and one white at the center of each square. Make two such assemblies at first.

Now prepare four squares, each of four blacks around a white. Attach two of these squares parallel to one of the initial planar assemblies, as follows. Let the corner of one square cover the central atom of one of the two squares in the first assembly, and the center of this new square cover the corner of the square of the first assembly. You will now have two parallel planes, one of joined squares, the next of two separate squares. This pattern of alternate layers is repeated throughout the crystal.

Fluorite and Antifluorite Structures: MX_2 or M_2X

The model consists of 14 white balls and 13 black balls, and is actually antifluorite if the white are metal. First construct a cube of whites around one black. The bond angle between two nearest neighbor bonds is 70.5 . Be sure the cube is symmetrical. Then assemble a similar cube, all but one edge. Attach this incomplete cube to the first cube so that an edge of the latter completes the former. In other words, an edge (two whites) is shared in common, and the two cubes should be aligned like stairs. The final structure, if extended far enough, becomes a regular assembly of such white cubes, sharing all six faces at the interior of the crystal, and having a black ball at the center of every other cube. Keeping this in mind, attach black balls to the two assembled cubes in such positions that they would occupy the centers of every other adjacent cube. Thus the more abundant element shows a coordination number of 8, the other, 4. Each atom is at the center of a cube of the other kind of atom, but half the cubes of the more abundant element surround a bole instead of an atom.

Rutile (TiO_2) Structure

The model contains 13 white balls and 20 black balls. In this crystal the coordination numbers of white and black are 6 and 3. You may begin by assembling two regular octahedra of black surrounding white, having one edge in common. Holding these so you see a plane of 6 blacks, in a verticle rectangle, attach one white to each of these six blacks to extend that rectangle to left and right. You now have a horizontal rectangle bordered on left and right edges by three white balls each. Now, perpendicular to this plane, connect two blacks to the three whites at each edge so as to bridge them. Turn the rectangle upside down and connect four more blacks just opposite the last four mentioned. To each of these, attach one white so that the white-black pair is perpendicular to the plane of the rectangle. Also bridge the two uppermost blacks of the original two octahedra by attaching one white. Looking down on the rectangle plane, you will now see five whites in a plane parallel to the rectangle and nearest to your eye: two at the left, two at the right, and one in the middle. You can now connect these whites together by a black at the center of each white triangle. The near plane will then consist of five whites and two blacks.

Layer Lattice: MX_2

The type of crystal model consists of 6 white and 13 black spheres, all the same size. Begin by connecting 6 blacks octahedrally to one white. Make a planar square of blacks around a white, and then attach the fifth and sixth black above and below the square. Let this assembly rest on a level surface so that it is stably supported on three blacks. The other three blacks will then form a triangle parallel to the base triangle but inverted in orientation. Then connect two whites to two of the base blacks so that each is also connected to a vertex black of the top triangle, and continue to extend the layer as far as desired. The entire layer is simply a combination of octahedra, all similarly oriented and sharing blacks in common. Each white ball, representing a metal atom, has 6 black balls, representing halogen atoms, coordinated to it. Each black ball is part of three octahedra in the layer and thus has a coordination number of 6. By different relative positions of such layers, modifications of layer lattices are produced.

Body-Centered Cubic Structure

Some of these have other forms also. In a model an atom has 8 closest neighbors at the corners of a cube surrounding it. At the centers of the six surrounding cubes are six more neighbors to the first, but these are about 15 per cent farther away.

Face-Centered Cubic Structure

This is also called ìcubic close packing.î To make a model in which one atom has 12 closest neighbors, attach four spheres around one, at the comers of a square. Then imagine two cubes to be constructed, one from each side of the plane of this square. Four faces of each cube are thus based on the original square and perpendicular to it. At the center of each of these eight faces is a sphere that touches the original central sphere. Thus are the 12 closest neighbors arranged.

Segen, J.C. Concise Dictionary of Modern Medicine. McGraw-Hill, 2006.

Stedmanís medical dictionary, illustrated. 27th ed. Philadelphia: Lippincott Williams & Wilkins, 2000.

Stetzenbach, L. D; Yates, M. V. Dictionary of environmental microbiology. San Diego: Academic Press, 2003.

The international classification of diseases; 9th revision, clinical modification; ICD 9 CM. Chicago: AMA Press, 2007.

USDA, NRCS. 2008. The PLANTS Database. http://plants.usda.gov (Oct 14, 2008). National Plant Data Center, Baton Rouge, LA.

Wilson, D.E. and Reeder, D.M., eds. Mammal species of the world. 3d ed. Baltimore: Johns Hopkins University Press, 2005.

Yanoff, M.; Duker, J. S., eds. Ophthalmology. 2d ed. St. Louis: Mosby, 2004.

Zipes, O.P. [and others], eds. Braunwaldís heart disease. 7th ed. Philadelphia: Elsevier-Saunders, 2005.

Index

L

M

N

O

P

Q

R

Other Text Books

1. Computer Education **(New)** 175/-
2. Teaching of Physics **(New)** 175/-
3. Media & Journalism **(New)** 195/-
4. Modern Education for New Generation **(New)** 175/-
5. Advanced Education Technology **(New)** 175/-
6. Comparative Education **(New)** 175/-
7. Introduction to Educational Research **(New)** 175/-
8. Advanced Educational Psychology **(New)** 175/-
9. Educational Administration & Origanisation Management **(New)** 175/-
10. Social Psychology **(New)** 225/-
11. Teaching of Commerce **(New)** 175/-
12. Educational Development & Technology **(New)** 175/-
13. Disaster Management **(New)** 175/-
14. Information Technology **(New)** 175/-
15. Human Resource Development **(New)** 175/-
16. Mass Media Communication **(New)** 225/-
17. Adult Education **(New)** 175/-
18. General Psychology **(New)** 175/-
19. Distance Education **(New)** 175/-
20. Teachers Education **(New)** 175/-
21. Educational Philosophy **(New)** 175/-
22. Science Teaching in Schools **(New)** 150/-
23. Indian Polity **(Revised New)** 295/-
24. New Comparative Government **(Revised New)** 275/-

Advance Study in the History of Modern India (PB)

25. (Volume-1: 1707-1803) 225/-
26. (Volume-2: 1803-1920) 325/-
27. (Volume-3: 1920-1947) 175/-
28. Handbook of Nutrition & Dietetics **(New)** 250/-
29. Development of Education in India 175/-